Learning
about
Learning

This book covers an area that is crucially important to people's lives yet which is rarely discussed in detail. Learning is a complex process which is in some ways unique to every individual. Yet there are themes that we can examine and understand as a step to making our learning more effective. The aim of this book is to help teachers and pupils learn more effectively; there are practical activities to use with pupils in classrooms and further material for teachers' workshops. Themes addressed include:

- motivating learners
- learning styles and strategies
- expressing opinions and beliefs
- learning in different contexts
- parents and learning
- developing a whole-school curriculum

Teachers, tutors, managers and all those who wish to see schools promote more effective learning will find this book invaluable.

Chris Watkins is head of the academic group 'Assessment, Guidance and Effective Learning' at the University of London Institute of Education. He is also course tutor to the MA in Effective Learning and the MA in School Development. **Eileen Carnell** tutors in areas including Effective Learning and Understanding Teachers' Professional Development at the University of London Institute of Education. **Caroline Lodge** is a lecturer in School Effectiveness and School Improvement at the University of London Institute of Education. **Patsy Wagner** is an Educational Psychologist who works collaboratively with teachers, pupils and parents in nursery, primary and secondary schools. **Caroline Whalley** is Assistant Director of Education in the London Borough of Ealing.

Learning about Learning

Resources for supporting effective learning

Chris Watkins, Eileen Carnell,
Caroline Lodge, Patsy Wagner
and Caroline Whalley

London and New York

First published 2000
by Routledge
11 New Fetter Lane, London EC4P 4EE

Simultaneously published in the USA and Canada
by Routledge
29 West 35th Street, New York, NY 10001

RoutledgeFalmer is an imprint of the Taylor & Francis Group

Typeset in ITC Garamond by
Keystroke, Jacaranda Lodge, Wolverhampton
Printed and bound in Great Britain by
TJ International Ltd, Padstow, Cornwall

British Library Cataloguing in Publication Data
A catalogue record for this book is available from the British Library

Library of Congress Cataloging in Publication Data
Learning about learning: resources for supporting effective learning / Chris Watkins . . . [et al.].
   p. cm.
   Includes bibliographical references (p.) and index.
   1. Learning. 2. Learning strategies. 3. Activity programs in education.
   I. Watkins, Chris.
   LB1060 .L395 2000
   370.15'23–dc21
                                                                  00-025184

ISBN 0-415-22349-0

'It's not that I haven't learnt much. It's just that I don't really understand what I'm doing'[1]

This quote from a pupil identifies the problem: zero learning about learning. We want this book to be part of the solution.

1 Rudduck J, Wallace G and Harris S (1995), '"It's not that I haven't learnt much. It's just that I don't understand what I'm doing": metacognition and secondary-school students', *Research Papers in Education*, 10(2): 253–271

Contents

This book is about learning

- ◆ Why bother with this book?
- ◆ What is in this book?
- ◆ How might you use it?
- ◆ Rationale
- ◆ Some permeating themes

Why bother with this book?

1   To help pupils and teachers learn more effectively. This happens when they
    have learned about their own learning, bringing:

    •   increased engagement in their own learning
    •   more positive feelings regarding their learning
    •   a better sense of ownership and responsibility
    •   improved use of feedback
    •   better links across their present contexts in school
    •   better preparation for a future in which learning will occur in a greater
        range of contexts.

2   To help pupils perform well. There is evidence that higher levels of perfor-
    mance are attained when a focus on learning about learning is added,
    whereas just focusing on performance can lead to worsening performance,
    through raised levels of anxiety, poorer use of feedback, and fewer links
    across learning contexts.
3   To help teachers and schools focus on learning, derive greater professional
    satisfaction, and make improved connections about learning between the
    different parts of the school.

What is in this book?

The book contains materials designed to engage teachers, pupils and parents in
activities that focus on learning about learning. Teachers, pupils and parents are
the key people in the learning process: each can improve learning through their
particular roles and responsibilities.

It offers ideas and activities with which you can experiment.

The overarching goal is to enhance language and understanding in aspects of
learning, and to enhance pupils' language in understanding their own learning.

Learning is too complex for there to be some simple quick-fix method.
Rather, these ideas support exploration and critical analysis of learning and
learning processes.

How might you use it?

Section A introduces key ideas and underlying themes.

Section B 'Workshop activities for teachers' can be used with any group of
teachers wanting to extend their understanding and try out appropriate practices. It might be a subject team, a year team, an interest group or even the whole
staff.

Section C 'Classroom activities to promote learning about learning' can
also be used in a range of contexts: subject lessons, group tutorials, individual
tutorials or any other context of academic tutoring. These activities can be used
by pupils to help each other, for example through cross-age peer tutoring.

Some of the activities from Sections C and D are interchangeable, with a few exceptions where the language may be inappropriate for pupils. Activities from both sections can also be used with parents and governors to develop understanding about learning.

Section D 'The wider context' contains ideas and resources to help make wider connections.

Materials from this book have already been used successfully with:

- groups of teachers from nursery, primary, secondary and special schools
- beginning teachers and their mentors
- educational psychologists
- university lecturers and local authority advisers.

Rationale

Why bother with learning about learning?

- To help us make sense of our present experiences of learning.
- To understand and extend our own learning, pupils' and others' learning.
- To help enhance a sense of responsibility about one's own learning.
- To promote co-operation and collaboration in learning experiences.
- To help the school develop coherence and congruence in its views about learning and its practices for learning.
- To plan more effectively for learning in the future.

Focusing on learning, not just on teaching

We often make an assumption that learning just happens as we teach. The term 'teaching and learning' is used often to describe 'teaching and teaching strategies', with little attention focused on learning. Many prevalent views of learning assume that it is a passive process of knowledge acquisition, with predictable and measurable outcomes. Definitions of learning contrast with those views.

> *Learning* [is] *that reflective activity which enables the learner to draw upon previous experience to understand and evaluate the present, so as to shape future action and formulate new knowledge.*[1]

Abbott's definition highlights the following:

- An active process of relating new meaning to existing meaning, involving the accommodation and assimilation of ideas, skills, thoughts and so on.

1 Abbott J (1994), *Learning Makes Sense: re-creating education for a changing future*, Letchworth: Education 2000

- The connections between past, present and future. These are not always made in a linear fashion: unlearning and relearning play their part.
- A process influenced by the use to which the learning might be put. All our learning might be varied and modified in future situations.

Preparing for a changed future

We need to promote a focus on learning about learning for the following reasons:

- The knowledge base in society is increasing rapidly and now doubles every four years.
- In a society increasingly organised around the processing of information more people need to be effective learners, and for a wider range of tasks.
- In a learning society, employment prospects relate more to the ability to enhance and transfer learning than the accumulation of qualifications.
- People need to learn in an increasing range of contexts, not just the compulsory ones.[1]

Effective learning and the role of meta-learning

Effective learning is promoted through:

- active learning
- collaborative learning
- responsibility in learning
- learning about learning, the major focus of this book.

We sometimes use the term 'meta-learning': it means learning about learning.

> *Learning is the process of creating knowledge by making sense of your experience.*
> *Meta-learning is the process of making sense of your experience of learning.*

Some permeating themes

Some themes and approaches underlie the activities that follow. They are, broadly, how we conceptualise learning, how we think learning is facilitated, and the role of activities in that process.

---

1 See the research review on 'effective learning' in Section E, at the end of this book.

About learning

Everyday views of learning vary. They include:[1]

- getting more knowledge
- memorising and reproducing
- applying facts or procedures
- understanding
- seeing something in a different way
- changing as a person.

At the beginning of this list are the more mechanical views of learning, but it moves to those which more clearly recognise that the learner is highly involved in making meaning and interpreting events. What has become increasingly clear from the research on learning is that learners are highly active in making meaning, including on occasions when those around them view the meanings as perfectly clear. This has increasingly been called a *constructivist* view of learning: the term indicates the *construction* of meaning which is at the heart of learning. Learners actively construct knowledge. They do this whether or not those around them are helping: at best their peers and teachers play a crucial role in helping the learner make sense.

About how learning is facilitated

If we recognise that learning is a process of constructing, no single approach to teaching will immediately follow. But certain elements will need to be present within the teaching approach. Whatever the classroom experience, learners need to process that experience in order to create knowledge, i.e. 'learn'. There are many tasks which may provide an opening to that processing (see for example the activity 'Terms for learning activities' on page 24).

We know that people do not learn from 'doing' alone. What is important is how connections are made - between experiences and between experiences and ideas.

> *It is not sufficient simply to have an experience in order to learn. Without reflecting upon this experience it may quickly be forgotten or its learning potential lost.*[2]

---

1 Marton F, Dall'Alba G and Beaty E (1993), 'Conceptions of learning', *International Journal of Educational Research*, 19(3): 277–300

2 Gibbs G (1988), *Learning by Doing: a guide to teaching and learning methods*, London: Further Education Unit

Key elements in the processing of experience include:

*   relating new meaning to existing meaning
*   reflecting on the current experience
*   using and applying the learning to future experiences.

People learn by adding variations to what they already know and do. In this way their understandings and actions become more complex and sophisticated. They do not simply delete previous understandings. Feedback by correction, which invites learners to substitute a new meaning for an old one, is often ineffective.

Throughout this book we use a series of four apparently simple words to indicate a learning process: Do → Review → Learn → Apply.

The role of activities in facilitating learning

It is useful to represent a learning cycle as shown in the diagram.[1]

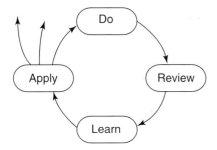

Teachers manage classrooms by managing activities. This cycle helps us to construct classroom activities which facilitate learning.

*   The *Do* phase could be one of a wide range of activities in the classroom: a problem to solve, a product to construct, a text to consider, a simulation to enact, a story to examine. Or it might be an experience outside the classroom, which is now to be considered and learned from.
*   The *Review* phase is a structured way of selecting and examining the important points. This is where experience begins to be processed.
*   The *Learn* phase is where pupils hear about a range of different approaches which might have been used, extract key ideas to make meaning of them, and identify what more they wish to learn. This is where connections are made, to ideas and to other experiences.
*   The *Apply* phase asks them to transfer their learning to situations they know, to plan some action and to set goals. The actions that are planned here could be either inside or outside the classroom. This is where the use of learning is highlighted. For many learners this is the key phase to maintain their momentum, motivation and sense of relevance.

---

1 Dennison B and Kirk R (1990), *Do Review Learn Apply: a simple guide to experiential learning*, Oxford: Blackwell

It is important that all four stages are supported in order to promote a full cycle of learning. We have found in using these activities that the review, learn and apply stages need significantly more time than the prompting activity itself. In this way we improve on the classroom scenario which can be all-too-common: a high degree of activity but a questionable degree of learning.

Classroom activities which are modelled on the above process will also engage the full range of learning styles as the cycle progresses. Pupils who have a strong preference and whose style may be described as Activists, Reflectors, Theorists and Pragmatists (see 'Learning styles – do we all learn in the same way?' on page 17) will come to the fore at different phases (as will teachers in the teacher activities).

The role of the teacher is to provide the necessary structures for pupils to progress through the learning cycle: setting up the initial tasks, structuring the review, promoting the learning and encouraging application. In all phases this requires the teacher to display skilled steering of the event, and to play a key role in making meaning and making connections. Teachers can make their specialist input through these processes. Facilitating learning through this cycle is, at its best, a highly structured (but still open-ended) process.

More often than not we portray the cycle as beginning with 'Do', but it can be entered at different points. For example a design class could start with a review of another product before pupils learn about key issues and plan to construct their own. Or a PSE (personal and social education) class could start with learning a new strategy before pupils plan to apply it themselves and review later.

Workshop activities for teachers

Which do you think is more prevalent –
teaching without learning
or
learning without teaching?

Pop this question on to an overhead projector with a group of colleagues and watch their faces as they puzzle about the issues it raises. It generates very useful starter discussion.

It is important too for the themes and activities that follow. We need to clarify that our focus is going to be on learning and we will temporarily separate it from teaching. This is not always easy to achieve. In part, this is because some commonly used terms like 'teaching and learning' are used rather like the phrase 'fish'n'chips', where the 'and' is almost forgotten, and the second half is taken for granted or deemed unproblematic.

Yet the contribution of the teaching profession is in the 'and' – in teaching for learning. There is little point in 'ritual teaching', without a focus on learning.

So if we first separate these two, we can then look more closely at how they are best put together.

WHERE'S THE LEARNER STARTING FROM?

The purpose of this activity is to recognise that learners come to a learning occasion in various 'states' regarding the learning at hand. It can be helpful to recognise these.

Look at the four stage model.[1] See whether it rings bells with your experience of learners, and the state they may be in at the start of some learning.

① *I don't know that I don't know how to do it* (unconscious incompetence)	② *I know that I don't know how to do it* (conscious incompetence)
③ *I know how to do it, and am aware of how I am doing it* (conscious competence)	④ *I know how to do it, but am no longer aware how* (unconscious competence)

It is suggested that state 2 is an ideal state at the start of a learning experience. Are there ways in which we can help learners to be in this state?

This activity will help you think about the way we progress through these states during the process of learning.

▷ **Do**   Think about a skill that you acquired easily, for example driving a car. Track through each of the stages as they occurred for you in that learning.

①	unconscious incompetence	I don't know that I don't know how to do it
②	conscious incompetence	I know that I don't know how to do it
③	conscious competence	I know how to do it, and am aware of how I am doing it
④	unconscious competence	I know how to do it, but am no longer aware how

▷ **Review**   Can you identify the characteristics of each stage?

▷ **Learn**   What helped you to progress through the stages?

1 Attributed to R Dubin; exact reference unknown.

▷ **Do**   Now think about a skill that you have had difficulty learning. Again, track through each of the stages as they occurred for you in that learning.

①	unconscious incompetence	I don't know that I don't know how to do it
②	conscious incompetence	I know that I don't know how to do it
③	conscious competence	I know how to do it, and am aware of how I am doing it
④	unconscious competence	I know how to do it, but am not aware how

▷ **Review**   Can you identify the characteristics of each stage?

▷ **Learn**   What made the progression between these stages difficult (or non-existent)?

▷ **Apply**   Are there any parallels between your experiences and the experiences of learners you work with? Do these ideas help understand their learning?

Can these ideas be used to improve their process of learning? How might you as a teacher utilise the idea that various of the learners in a class may be at all four of the stages in relation to a particular learning?

LEARNING AND 'MOTIVATION'

The purpose of this activity is to consider the orientations of learners, the effects of these orientations and the influence of school.

Some uses of the term 'motivation' can get us stuck. For example, the idea that some learners 'have more of it in them' than others can lead us to a deficit view of some learners, and thence a lack of appropriate challenge.

Other uses of the term help us see that different learners have different styles of approaching achievement-related activities. We then recognise how much the tasks and contexts influence motivation.

Dweck identified different motivational styles (learning orientation and performance orientation) and their characteristics.[1]

Learning orientation	Performance orientation
a belief that effort leads to success	*a belief that ability leads to success*
a belief in one's ability to improve and learn	*a concern to be judged as able, and a concern to perform*
a preference for challenging tasks	*satisfaction from doing better than others or succeeding with little effort*
derives satisfaction from personal success at difficult tasks	*emphasis on interpersonal competition normative standards, public evaluation*
applies problem-solving and self-instructions when engaged in task	*helplessness: evaluates self negatively when task is difficult*

The performance orientation is much linked to learners who say 'I can't do it' when things get tough, whereas people with a learning orientation can talk themselves through the difficulties they meet, including difficulties in a learning process.

▷ **Do**   On your own, think of two learners you know who differ on this dimension.

▷ **Review**   How do these two learners differ in their approach to learning tasks? Are there ways you have found to engage each of them?

Exchange your examples with a colleague.

---

1 Dweck C (1986), 'Motivational processes affecting learning', *American Psychologist*, 41: 1040–1048

☞ **Learn**   What principles inform how you can engage a learner with performance orientation?

☞ **Apply**   There are significant disadvantages to the performance orientation. In what ways can you help someone move more towards a learning orientation:

- through the tasks you devise?
- through the assessment and feedback you offer?
- through occasions when you help learners learn from each other?

The effect of context on learners' orientation

☞ **Do**   Think about and identify what aspects of school practice promote the differing learners' orientations. Make some notes on the chart.

	Promoting a learning orientation	Promoting a performance orientation
School and wider context		
Classroom practice		
Assessment and guidance practice		

▷ **Review**   Exchange with colleagues and discuss the various points which you have made.

▷ **Learn**   What are the aspects of your practice which you agree on?

▷ **Apply**   Identify some ways in which your school practice could promote more of a learning orientation.

Discuss how these developments might be implemented.

LEARNING STYLES – DO WE ALL LEARN IN THE SAME WAY?

This activity helps you to consider the notion of learning style, and how the notion can help us as teachers.

First, the questionnaire gives an indication of the preferred style(s) you presently adopt.[1]

Learning Styles Questionnaire

PETER HONEY AND ALAN MUMFORD

This questionnaire is designed to find out your preferred learning style(s).

Over the years you have probably developed learning 'habits' that help you benefit more from some experiences than from others. Since you are probably unaware of this, this questionnaire will help you pinpoint your present learning and decision-making preferences.

There is no time limit to this questionnaire. It will probably take you 10–15 minutes. The accuracy of the results depends on how honest you can be. There are no right or wrong answers.

If you agree more than you disagree with a statement put a tick by it. If you disagree more than you agree put a cross. Be sure to mark each item with either a tick or a cross. You may find that some of your answers contradict others. Do not worry about this apparent inconsistency.

1 I often take reasonable risks, if I feel it justified   ☐ ☐
2 I tend to solve problems using a step-by-step approach, avoiding any fanciful ideas   ☐ ☐
3 I have a reputation for having a no-nonsense direct style   ☐ ☐
4 I often find that actions based on feelings are as sound as those based on careful thought and analysis   ☐ ☐
5 The key factor in judging a proposed idea or solution is whether it works in practice   ☐ ☐
6 When I hear about a new idea or approach I like to start working out how to apply it in practice as soon as possible   ☐ ☐
7 I like to follow a self-disciplined approach, establish clear routines and logical thinking patterns   ☐ ☐
8 I take pride in doing a thorough, methodical job   ☐ ☐
9 I get on best with logical, analytical people, and less well with spontaneous, 'irrational' people   ☐ ☐

---

1 Honey P and Mumford A (1989), 'Trials and tribulations', *Guardian*, 19 December

10 I take care over the interpretation of data available to me, and avoid jumping to conclusions ☐ ☐

11 I like to reach a decision carefully after weighing up many alternatives ☐ ☐

12 I'm attracted more to new, unusual ideas than to practical ones ☐ ☐

13 I dislike situations that I cannot fit into a coherent pattern ☐ ☐

14 I like to relate my actions to a general principle ☐ ☐

15 In meetings I have a reputation of going straight to the point, no matter what others feel ☐ ☐

16 I prefer to have as many sources of information as possible – the more data to consider the better ☐ ☐

17 Flippant people who don't take things seriously enough usually irritate me ☐ ☐

18 I prefer to respond to events on a spontaneous, flexible basis rather than plan things out in advance ☐ ☐

19 I dislike very much having to present my conclusions under the time pressure of tight deadlines, when I could have spent more time thinking about the problem ☐ ☐

20 I usually judge other people's ideas principally on their practical merits ☐ ☐

21 I often get irritated by people who want to rush headlong into things ☐ ☐

22 The present is much more important than thinking about the past or future ☐ ☐

23 I think that decisions based on a thorough analysis of all the information are sounder than those based on intuition ☐ ☐

24 In meetings I enjoy contributing ideas to the group, just as they occur to me ☐ ☐

25 On balance I tend to talk more than I should, and ought to develop my listening skills ☐ ☐

26 In meetings I get very impatient with people who lose sight of the objectives ☐ ☐

27 I enjoy communicating my ideas and opinions to others ☐ ☐

28 People in meetings should be realistic, keep to the point, and avoid indulging in fancy ideas and speculations ☐ ☐

29 I like to ponder many alternatives before making up my mind ☐ ☐

30 Considering the way my colleagues react in meetings, I reckon on the whole I am more objective and unemotional ☐ ☐

31 At meetings I'm more likely to keep in the background, than to take the lead and do most of the talking ☐ ☐

32 On balance I prefer to do the listening than the talking ☐ ☐

33 Most times I believe the end justifies the means ☐ ☐

34 Reaching the group's objectives and targets should take precedence over individual feelings and objections ☐ ☐

35 I do whatever seems necessary to get the job done ☐ ☐

36 I quickly get bored with methodical, detailed work ☐ ☐

37 I am keen on exploring the basic assumptions, principles and theories underpinning things and events ☐ ☐

38 I like meetings to be run on methodical lines, sticking to laid down agendas ☐ ☐

39 I steer clear of subjective or ambiguous topics ☐ ☐

40 I enjoy the drama and excitement of a crisis ☐ ☐

How to score:

For each of your answers to the questionnaire, transfer the tick into the appropriate boxes, and total them across each row.

1	4	12	18	22	24	25	27	36	40	Total: Activist	

8	10	11	16	19	21	23	29	31	32	Total: Reflector	

2	7	9	13	14	17	30	37	38	39	Total: Theorist	

3	5	6	15	20	26	28	33	34	35	Total: Pragmatist	

To make the comparisons below, double the number you scored in each category.

Ring on this chart and join up.   Here is an example:

Activist	Reflector	Theorist	Pragmatist	
20	20	20	20	
19				
18		19		
17			19	
16	19	18		Very strong preference
15			18	
14		17		
13	18	16	17	
12	17	15	16	
	16			Strong preference
11	15	14	15	
10	14	13	14	
9	13	12	13	
8				Moderate preferance
7	12	11	12	
6	11	10	11	
5	10	9	10	Low preference
4	9	8	9	
3	8	7	8	
	7	6	7	
	6	5	6	
2	5	4	5	
	4		4	Very low preference
1	3	3	3	
	2	2	2	
	1	1	1	
0	0	0	0	

Jack Straw, former student activist, MP for Blackburn, and currently Home Secretary

▷ **Review**   Is the result similar to or different from what you might have expected?

▷ **Learn**   How does your profile of styles look?

Did you have a strong preference for one style? For more than one?

Now read the characteristics that are suggested for each style.

The characteristics of each learning style are suggested as follows.

- *Activists* involve themselves fully in new experiences. They are open-minded, not sceptical, and this tends to make them enthusiastic about anything new. Their philosophy is 'I'll try anything once'. They tend to act first and consider the consequences afterwards. They tackle problems by brainstorming. They are gregarious people constantly involving themselves with others, but, in doing so, they seek to centre all activities around themselves.

- *Reflectors* like to stand back to ponder experiences and observe them from many different perspectives. The thorough collection and analysis of data about experiences and events is what counts, so they tend to postpone reaching definitive conclusions for as long as possible. Their philosophy is to be cautious. They prefer to take a back seat in meetings and discussions. They listen to others and get the drift of discussions before making their own points.

- *Theorists* adapt and integrate observations into complex theories. They like to analyse and synthesise. They are keen on basic assumptions, principles, theories, models and systems thinking. Their philosophy prizes rationality and logic. Questions they frequently ask are 'How does this fit with that?' and 'What are the basic assumptions?'

- *Pragmatists* are keen on trying out ideas, theories and techniques to see if they work in practice. They positively search out new ideas and take the first opportunity to experiment with applications. They are the sort of people who return from courses brimming with new ideas that they want to try out in practice. They like to get on with things and act quickly and confidently on ideas. They are impatient with ruminating discussion.

▷ **Review**   Critically analyse these descriptions and adapt them to your own knowledge about yourself as a learner.

Remember that this is not about 'personality' – you can have more than one style and your style can change. You may find that you adopt a different style for different situations.

Identify occasions when you have adopted the style of an activist, a reflector, a theorist and a pragmatist.

Of the learning styles where you show a strong preference, do the descriptions highlight important aspects of your approach to learning? Does this relate to a general picture or is it specific to certain contexts? Of the learning styles which you prefer least, are important aspects of your approach highlighted?

☞ Learn

Do your present preferences for learning reflect your style? For example:

- activists may prefer groupwork or projects with others
- reflectors may prefer creating reviews or critiques
- theorists may prefer reading and independent research
- pragmatists may prefer experimental approaches.

Can you identify both strengths and weaknesses for your preferred style? And for your less preferred style?

☞ Apply

Knowing this about yourself, how could you begin to plan to extend the range of learning styles you use and when you use them? For each of your two least preferred styles, suggest one way in which you could develop it in your work.

What support do you need to help you extend your range of styles?

TEACHERS AND THEIR PUPILS' LEARNING STYLES

This activity helps teachers to think about how they might use the notion of learning style, by thinking through a range of options. If you have taken the time to illuminate your own learning style preferences using the preceding pages, we hope that you are less likely to fall into a common trap in using these ideas: categorising people as one type or another. This is an oversimplification which is contrary to our educational goal.

So what positive use is the notion of learning style?

1 We as teachers can increase our awareness of the repertoire of styles that our learners adopt.

   Anything which helps us focus on learning can be useful. Effective teachers focus on their pupils' perspective on learning. The link between preferred learning style and types of activities engaged in can be important to consider.

2 We can match learning tasks to learners.

   Given the usual size and composition of classroom groups, this use is most likely when planning work with a small group of exceptional learners. Everyday classroom managers do not find it feasible, a fact which may explain what some enthusiasts have described as an unwillingness on the part of schools to adapt to pupil style.

3 We can structure activities so that they reach a wider range of learners.

   This use does not require the administration of diagnostic instruments to classes of learners. Instead, it points to the use of learning methods which engage each learning style at some point in their overall process. For example activists, reflectors, theorisers and pragmatists would each come to the fore at different stages of a Do–Review–Learn–Apply cycle.

   Such an approach would also clarify the rationale for taking styles seriously – that a range of learning styles is important for each pupil's future as a learner. It may also contribute to the goal of extending every pupil's learning-style repertoire.

4 We can help learners understand their present repertoire of styles and how to extend their approaches to learning.

   That is what the pupil activities in this book are for. They might be used in a range of contexts: classroom reviews and planning discussions, as well as in smaller-scale events such as tutoring and mentoring. As teachers we can build confidence in learners as they experiment with different styles.

☞ **Do**   Consider the above four uses of the notion of learning style.

☞ **Review**   Are there others you would add?

Which of the above have you used? With what impact?

☞ **Learn**   Exchange your experience of use with some colleagues.

Find out in detail how any of you have used the notion of preferred learning styles, and identify how it has been used for positive impact.

☞ **Apply**   Anticipate some of the forces which may hinder you from positive use of these ideas, and how you will tackle those hindrances.

Identify an appropriate occasion and plan how you will use that occasion to extend your use of the idea.

You might consider using the activity 'Learning-style questionnaire' (see page 57).

TERMS FOR LEARNING ACTIVITIES

The purpose of this activity is to extend our vocabulary for learning activities, and to reflect on their relationship to different learning styles.

Here is a list of words for some of the learning activities that take place in classrooms. Read them and then make your own sense of them with a colleague.

listening   *creating*

reciting   *reading*   *modelling*   *writing*

attending   *making*   *thinking*   *categorising*

telling   *reviewing*   *analysing*   *describing*

planning   *questioning*   *re-planning*   *presenting*

drafting   *rejecting*   *discussing*   *debating*   *judging*

critiquing   *letting go*   *brainstorming*   *deciding*

deconstructing   *relating*   *communicating*   *evaluating*

prioritising   *solving*   *receiving feedback*

connecting   *integrating*   *giving feedback*

negotiating   *synthesising*   *experimenting*

rehearsing   *applying*

People have different profiles of preferred learning styles (see pages 17–21). Any class or group of learners will include a range of styles, and the activities we use to promote learning would best engage all four styles.

▷ **Do**   Working in pairs, select learning activities from the above array which suit each of the learning styles:

Activist   *Reflector*   *Theorist*   *Pragmatist*

▷ **Review**   Did you find some words to fit each style?

Did some words fit more than one style?

Was it hard to find some activities to fit any of the learning styles?

Did you consider adding other words? Which? Why?

▷ **Learn**   Now create combinations of learning activities which would engage all four styles. For example:

drafting → critiquing → analysing → experimenting

Exchange your ideas with some other pairs of colleagues.

▷ **Apply**   Review the present profile of learning activities in your classroom, and see whether any of your new combinations would help to engage more learners.

LEARNING IN SCHOOL AND OUT

This activity will help you to consider learning in different contexts, and consider improvements to learning in school.

A contrast has been made between learning in school and out of school.[1]

In school	Out of school
decontextualised	has real context
second-hand	first-hand
need motivating	comes easily
individualistic	co-operative, shared
assessed by others	self-assessed
formal structure	few structures

There is growing evidence that:

- schooling may not contribute in a direct and obvious way to performance outside school
- knowledge acquired outside school is not always used to support in-school learning.

Schooling is coming to look increasingly isolated from the rest of what we do.[2]

☞ **Do** In a group, discuss how you see the differences between learning in school and out of school.

☞ **Review** What contrasts and similarities did you find between you? Did any patterns emerge?

☞ **Learn** What insights or new understandings have you gained?

Resnick suggests three key features of successful programmes for acquiring learning skills in and out of school:

- engaging in shared work and joint tasks, where skills are meaningful for the problem at hand
- making hidden processes overt, for example through encouraging pupil observation and commentary
- organising work around particular knowledge and problems, rather than general abilities.

---

1 Biggs JB and Moore PJ (1993), *The Process of Learning*, 3rd edn, Englewood Cliffs NJ: Prentice-Hall
2 Resnick LB (1987), 'Learning in school and out', *Educational Researcher*, 16(9): 13–40

▷ **Apply**   Consider ways in which school learning can be made more like everyday learning. What would be changed?

Where, when and how in your teaching can you add some of the characteristics you have identified?

What implications do you see for supporting learning in school?

A CLOSED PROBLEM?

This activity introduces a major theme: your thinking about your thinking.

☞ **Do**   Try to solve this problem in your head:

> *How much is half of two plus two?*

☞ **Review**   What happened when you did this? For example:

- Did you find that you were talking to yourself?
- Did you see the numbers in your head?
- Did you visualise the parts of the problem in some way?
- Did you choose to halve the first 'two' or to add the 'twos' first?
- Did you have a block of any kind? Did you resolve it? How?
- How did you feel when you were set this problem?
- How did you feel about solving this problem?
- Did you notice that you were comparing yourself with others?
- When you found a solution, did you want to attract 'teacher'?

☞ **Learn**   Thinking about your thinking is a crucial step towards learning about your learning. When you are aware of your thinking you can evaluate it, and start to notice your strategies. Being aware of the approaches you use helps you reflect on them and review them.[1]

Include your thinking about the problem as well as your thinking about the situation you were in while doing it.

☞ **Apply**   How would you use the understanding you have gained to help your pupils start to explore such problems and think about their strategies?

What problems which you set pupils might be similar and which you could use to promote consciousness about learning? N.B. There are two possible right answers that we know of to this *closed* problem:

$$\frac{2+2}{2} = 2 \qquad \frac{2+2}{2} = 3 \qquad \text{(There might be more!)}$$

---

1 Costa AL (1984), 'Mediating the metacognitive', *Educational Leadership*, 42 (Nov.): 57–62. Note: metacognition is a very important high-level process in which humans engage: it is thinking about thinking.

THE SIX ORANGES PUZZLE

This activity can help us look at how we solve problems and how we get past any blocks that we might meet.[1]

▷ **Do**   You are about to be presented with a problem. Try to solve it in whatever way works for you, and also try to *notice what happens to your thinking* as you try.

There are six oranges in the bag.

How can you give these six children an orange each and still have one left in the bag?

If you think you have arrived at a solution, *don't tell anyone for the moment,* but try to remember the process you went through to get it. [3-5 minutes]

In groups, anyone who feels that they have a solution should explain it and find out whether their colleagues accept it. [3 minutes]

On your own, note down the thoughts that went through your mind as you tried to solve the puzzle - whether you came up with an answer or not. [3 minutes]

▷ **Review**   How did anyone who found a solution manage to do it?

What thinking did they use? Why did it work?

How did anyone who did not find a solution manage not to?

What thinking did they use? Why did it not work? [10 minutes]

▷ **Learn**   Some people who got a solution might have 'broken the rules' in other people's terms. They bought another orange, they gave the last child the orange in a bag, they gave an orange and then took it back, and so on. (There are lots of solutions once you start this!)

---

1   Six oranges puzzle is developed from Watkins C (1989), *Your New School: tutorial resources for Year One*, Harlow: Longman

Some people who did not get a solution might have 'had a block'. They might have thought 'This is maths – I'm no good at it' or 'I hate these kinds of things' or 'There's a trick being played on me' or 'This hasn't really got an answer at all'.

In small groups find further examples of the 'Breakthroughs and Blocks' and try to spot what you have to do to break through. [10 minutes]

Apply

Does this puzzle remind you of other situations you have been in? Which ones?

Is there any new way you can try to get a breakthrough? [5 minutes]

FIRST STEPS IN LEARNING ABOUT LEARNING

The purpose of this activity is to take the first step in learning about your learning, which is thinking about your learning. From there, improvements may follow. [This activity could take 40 minutes]

First, consider the following statement from a pupil:

> *It's not that I haven't learnt much. It's just that I don't really understand what I'm doing.*[1]

Does this statement ring bells for you? It describes a situation where no meta-learning has occurred. Learning is impoverished. The person has not thought about or understood *what they are doing* in order to learn.

▷ **Do**

Spend time working on your own. Think of a learning situation, recently, when you really understood your own learning. That is, you understood what you were doing in order to learn. Identify and note down what you were thinking about your learning as you were learning. [3–5 minutes]

Then, in pairs, exchange your ideas with another person.

▷ **Review**

Continue in your pair to explore the following. [10 minutes]

For each of you, what were the different aspects of your thinking about your learning that you have been reflecting on? What words and processes came to mind? Do they relate to:

- your *purposes* for learning
- the *strategies* you were using
- the *effects* of your learning
- your *feelings* while you were learning
- the *context* of your learning – including the physical environment, the social environment and atmosphere, the timing, materials and resources, how you used these and how you had impact on them

or combinations of these?

▷ **Learn**

Continue working in pairs. Identify any ways in which your thinking about your learning *helped* your learning. [5 minutes]

---

1 Rudduck J, Wallace G and Harris S (1995), '"It's not that I haven't learnt much. It's just that I don't understand what I'm doing": metacognition and secondary-school students', *Research Papers in Education*, 10(2): 253–271

▷ **Apply**   On your own, think of a learning situation where your learning is not going so well, one in which you would like to
improve your learning. Reflect on:

- your *purposes* for learning
- the *strategies* you were using
- the *effects* of your learning
- your *feelings* while you were learning
- the *context* of your learning.

Note down how you could influence any of these aspects so as
to enhance your learning. [5 minutes]

   Then, in a small group, exchange the ideas and plans you
have each had for using these thoughts to enhance your own
learning. Develop further ideas together. [10 minutes]

PROMOTING LEARNING ABOUT LEARNING, OR META-LEARNING

The purpose of this activity is to clarify meta-learning, how it might be promoted, and ways of promoting meta-learning with pupils.

▷ **Do**   Spend some time working on your own, considering the statements and diagrams that follow. [5 minutes]

The learning of many ideas, skills and 'content' is promoted through a process of action and reflection which we can portray as shown in the diagram.

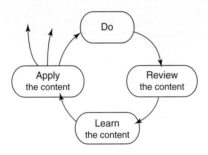

We can call this the first phase: content learning.

When learning occurs, or even sometimes when it does not, we can also reflect on the same action, but now focusing on learning about the learning.

We can portray this as shown in the diagram.

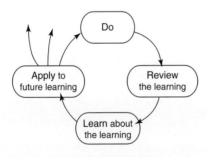

We can call this the second phase: learning about learning, or meta-learning.

Learning is the process of creating knowledge by making sense of experience.

Meta-learning is the process of making sense of your experience of learning.

▷ **Review**   Work in pairs: exchange examples you have come across of meta-learning, distinguishing it from content learning. [10 minutes]

☞ **Learn**　Then, in pairs, explore your examples further and try to identify what learnings about learning were achieved. [10 minutes]

What were the key elements that helped?

☞ **Apply**　Can you identify some ways of promoting meta-learning with others?

The language of meta-learning

If you ask people to tell you about their learning, they often tell you what they have learned. They focus on outcome, and have few ways of describing the process.

In order to learn about learning we need a language to help us describe the elements that influence our learning. We can then learn about learning by reviewing our experiences of learning and focusing explicitly on these influential elements.

☞ **Do**　Consider the headings offered in the diagram. They aim to highlight influential elements in our learning.

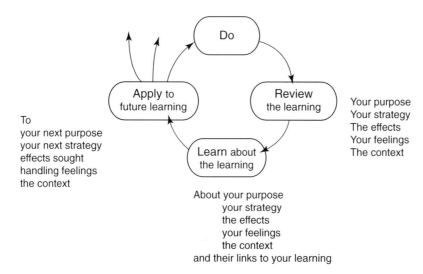

☞ **Review**　Work in pairs: does your previous learning about your learning highlight similar elements (purpose, strategy, effects, feelings, context)?

Are there others you would add? [10 minutes]

☞ **Learn**　Then, in pairs: if you had used the cycle

Do → Review → Learn → Apply

and the elements – purpose, strategy, effects, feelings, context – could your earlier experience of learning about learning have been improved?

What additional insights might you have gained? [10 minutes]

▷ **Apply**   In pairs and then in a group, develop a list of ideas for practices which could promote your pupils' learning about their learning.

How could these ideas be used routinely so that they are embedded in classroom and school practice?

PROMPTS TO PROMOTE THE STAGES IN A CYCLE OF META-LEARNING

This set of prompts could be used:

- alone by a learner who is wanting to develop their learning about their learning
- together by a learner and someone who is helping them learn about their learning.

☞ **Review** *Purposes*   What purpose did you have in mind?

- To 'meet requirements'?
- To beat others?
- To 'get through'?
- Out of interest?
- To please others?

Strategy   How did you set about it (the learning)?

- What did you do?
- Did you alter as you went?
- What strategies did you *not* use?

Effects   Did your results fulfil your purpose?

- What helped/hindered in the learning?
- What went well/not well? Did you meet any blocks?
- How did it progress over time? Thinking, feeling, strategy . . .

Feelings   What did you enjoy/not enjoy in the learning?

- What risks did you take?
- What surprises did you have?

Context   Did you work with others?

- What influences on your learning did you notice?
- What interactions with other people did you notice, find helpful/unhelpful?

☞ **Learn**   What new understandings about your learning have emerged?

- About how your *purpose*/motive influenced your learning?
- About your view of learning?

- About an (effective) *strategy*?
- About how you dealt with 'blocks'? 'How you talked yourself through'?

- About the main *effects* of your learning?
- About the main influences on those effects?

- Your management of *feelings*?
- About the effect of feelings on your learning and your strategy?

- About how you made use of /influenced the *context*?
- About how this learning connects/compares with other learning, other contexts?

▷ **Apply**
- How will you set your *purpose* next time?
- What changes about your view of learning do you need to enact?
- What *strategy* will you experiment with? Which will you avoid?
- What approach to blocks next time? (How will you talk yourself through?)
- What *effects* do you seek?
- How will you manage your *feelings* next time?
- How can you see things differently next time?
- How will you influence the *context* so that it works for you?
- What extra feedback will you seek?
- What extra things do you intend to notice?

WHAT IS AN EFFECTIVE LEARNER LIKE?

Effective learners have gained understanding of the processes necessary to become effective learners.[1] Effective learning 'is that which actively involves the pupil in meta-cognitive processes of planning, monitoring and reflecting'.[2]

Effective learners, therefore:

- are both active and strategic
- are skilled in co-operation
- are able to develop goals
- understand their own learning.

Effective learners have a repertoire of strategies, the skill of selecting appropriately from them, and the orientation to learn more. Even on occasions when the learning context may not be effective, such learners are able to take themselves through the process of learning in a private way.

☞ **Do**   Think about learners you know, especially ones whom you regard as effective. They might be colleagues, pupils or friends. Include yourself in your considerations.

☞ **Review**   Which of the above four features do you recognise:

- in yourself?
- in colleagues?

Have you already got effective/strategic learners among your pupils?

Which features of effective learners do you recognise in classes you teach?

Which features are less common?

☞ **Learn**   Work with colleagues to identify similarities and differences in what you have noticed about effective learners.

Are there any trends that reflect on your school?

1 Nisbet J and Shucksmith J (1986), *Learning Strategies*, London: Routledge; Novak JD and Gowin DB (1984), *Learning How to Learn*, Cambridge: Cambridge University Press; Biggs, J (ed.) (1991), *Teaching for Learning: the view from cognitive psychology*, Melbourne: Australian Council for Educational Research (ACER)

2 Biggs JB and Moore PJ (1993), *The Process of Learning*, 3rd edn, Englewood Cliffs NJ: Prentice-Hall

☞ **Apply**

Are there any implications for your practice? Will you adapt or amend your teaching approach in the light of your findings?

How could you use the four features, i.e. effective learners

- are both active and strategic
- are skilled in co-operation
- are able to develop goals
- understand their own learning

to help you think about individual learners and what they need to develop into more effective learners?

REFLECTING ON YOUR LEARNING

For busy teachers, there can be precious few reflective moments. As Jean Rudduck put it:

> The cycles of routines that the rhythms of institutional life seem to require inevitably lead practitioners to reconstruct each day in its own image, making it difficult to step back, and to look, even briefly, with the eyes of a stranger.[1]

Creating an informal format and a record for your reflections can increase and enhance the process. That is a reflective journal on learning.

What has reflection got to do with learning?

Reflection and learning are closely linked. Reflection helps move the learner into further learning.[2] It is the first step in the cycle, which helps us learn from whatever we do.

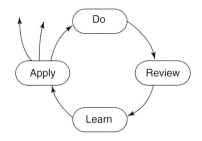

How can I reflect?

There is no one method which works for everyone.

One way to reflect on your learning is by discussing it with someone else, such as a colleague. The thoughts that are set off by these conversations may also develop while you are alone.

Writing down your thoughts also promotes reflection and learning. A journal which helps you think about your work and what you are learning from it can be both satisfying and energising.

People often use a diary type of format. Like a diary, a journal is usually private.

Different people of course use different styles, write in their journals with different and varying frequency, and sometimes do not use them for several

---

1 Rudduck J (1988), 'The ownership of change as a basis for teachers' professional learning', in Calderhead J (ed.) *Teachers' Professional Learning*, Brighton: Falmer Press

2 Boud D, Keogh R and Martin D (eds) (1985), *Reflection: turning experience into learning*, London: Kogan Page

weeks or months. You need to think of your journal as a tool to help your learning not as a duty.

You could use a learning journal to reflect on:

- a particular development in which you are involved
- a particular lesson or task
- connections between different activities or lessons
- your reactions to something you have read
- important incidents in your learning
- any blocks you come across in your learning
- what you are learning about your approaches to learning
- what you are learning about your learning
- the changes you are making
- what you are learning about the way you are making changes.

Reflection can be thought of as an internal conversation. That is why it is often useful to pose some questions and try to answer them, to get the process going.

The following suggested questions may help promote reflection on your learning, its content and process.

Content

- What you are learning: *e.g. what did I learn about this? What was new? What do I need to learn now?*
- Progress in your learning: *e.g. how have things changed? How am I getting on with my plan?*

Process

- Why – your purpose in learning: *e.g. what is important to me in this work and why?*
- How – your strategy in learning: *e.g. which way did I go about this task?*
- Results – effects you noticed: *e.g. what helped me in this learning and what got in the way?*
- Feelings involved in the learning: *e.g. how did I feel when I started the task and how did that influence what I did?*
- Context issues: *e.g. how did I work with the group on a task? What resources were useful? Did I influence the context?*

> *What supports the writing of your learning journal?*
> *What inhibits the writing of your learning journal?*

With these starters, and keeping the *Do → Review → Learn → Apply* cycle in mind, you are likely to explore a fruitful range of aspects in your learning and its use.

DEVELOPING META-LEARNING IN YOUR SCHOOL

Now that you have explored the meaning and importance of learning about learning (page 32) what might you have to consider when developing it in your school?

When we consider making any sort of change, it can be useful to view the present situation as a balance between two types of forces (see diagram).

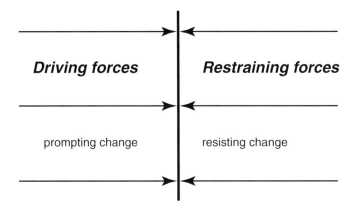

'Forces' could be a range of things or the lack of them: practices, resources, skills, policies, understanding, people's view of themselves and of others, and so on.

Successful change attempts to address both the promoting and the restraining forces, increasing the former at the same time as decreasing the latter.

You might find it useful to think in turn about the elements in the model:

* What aspects of the learner characteristics promote/restrain meta-learning?
* What aspects of the teaching characteristics promote/restrain meta-learning?
* What aspects of the teaching-learning processes promote/restrain meta-learning?

and so on

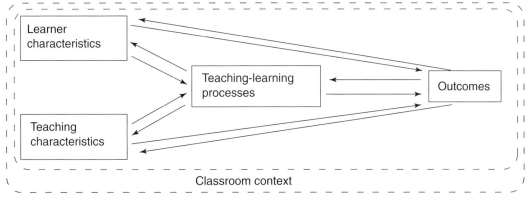

▷ **Do**   Carry out a force-field analysis, noting down the aspects which promote meta-learning and those which restrain meta-learning in your school.

Note your ideas on the chart.

	Promoting meta-learning	*Restraining meta-learning*
Learner characteristics		
Teaching characteristics		
Teaching-learning processes		
Outcomes		
Context		

▷ **Review**   Take one area at a time. Consider the actions that would need to be taken to both enhance the promoting forces and decrease the effect of the restraining forces. Note them down.

When you have covered a few areas, prioritise the actions that are emerging. Identify actions for yourself, your team and the whole school.

▷ **Learn**   'Innovation requires a Good Idea, Initiative, and a Few Friends'.

Select the actions that are most likely to succeed.

Identify who you will work with to make them happen.

▷ **Apply**   Make a plan of your next actions.

Check that they are achievable, believable and controllable (by you).

Decide when you will review how the plan has proceeded.

Classroom activities to promote learning about learning

- ◆ Introduction
- ◆ How do we learn best?
- ◆ Time line of learning experiences
- ◆ Learning strategy questionnaire
- ◆ Learning styles questionnaire
- ◆ Beliefs about success
- ◆ Handling feelings in learning
- ◆ Defences against learning
- ◆ Explaining your success
- ◆ Learning – in school and out
- ◆ Learning situations – in school
- ◆ Learning situations – beyond school
- ◆ Review of learning check list
- ◆ Keeping a learning file
- ◆ Back to the future: exploring and planning possible routeways to your preferred future

Classroom activities to promote learning about learning

This section contains activities for pupils. The focus is on learning *about* learning. The purpose is to help pupils explore, reflect on and learn about the processes of learning.

The principles about learners and learning which underlie these activities are as follows:

1   An effective learner is a person who has gained an understanding of the processes involved in learning and is able to apply that understanding in learning across a wide range of contexts.
2   Effective learning involves processes of:

   - making connections about what has been learned in different contexts
   - reflecting about one's own learning and learning strategies
   - exploring how the learning contexts have played a part in making the learning effective
   - setting further learning goals
   - engaging with others in learning.

The activities in this section are not, therefore, related to particular subject areas but, rather, to the processes of learning, and of learning in different contexts. The overall aim is to enhance pupil learning across a range of different contexts.

The activities are structured to have a sequence and a progression. They have been designed to be pupil and teacher friendly and could be used with secondary or junior pupils. They would need adaptation for younger learners.

When planning for effective learning, the tasks and processes need to promote:

   - active learning
   - collaborative learning
   - responsibility in learning
   - learning about learning.

In order to achieve this the activities are carefully structured around stages in the learning cycle.

☞ **Do**   The learners engage in a variety of tasks and processes which require reflection, collaboration and group work.

☞ **Review**   The learners reflect on the activity and evaluate the cognitive and affective aspects which may have helped or hindered their learning both as individuals and as part of the group.

☞ **Learn**   The learners process the insights and understandings which emerged in the review stage about the learning. These may touch on:

why	*purposes in learning*
how do	*strategies in learning*
what result	*effects in learning*
how feel	*feelings in learning*
when, who with, where	*context of learning*

This then leads to learners developing new strategies and/or revising their old strategies for learning.

▷ **Apply**   Learners reflect on and make plans about using their new or revised strategies in different learning contexts.

The role of the teacher is crucial in these activities in promoting effective learning:

▷ **Do**   The teacher encourages and supports the learners in engaging actively in the activities, tasks and processes.

▷ **Review**   The teacher facilitates the reflection, discussion and feedback and supports the emergence of new understandings and insights and the learners' evaluation of strategies.

▷ **Learn**   The teacher helps the pupils to make the learning explicit, drawing out the insights and understandings that emerged in the review stage, helping to compare and contrast present strategies and how they can be revised and developed for the next stage.

▷ **Apply**   The teacher helps the learners to plan future action differently in the light of new understanding, by promoting transfer of learning, planning of strategies for specific situations and contexts, and goal-setting.

Teachers will find that the activities work best when they have been tried out by the teacher first. Section B and section C are linked and complementary. Consequently, some activities from section B could also be used with pupils: activities from section C could also be used with teachers. This will help teachers become familiar with the material, assess the time it will take and work out how best to use it with the group of learners they have in mind. We expect that each activity will take around 45 minutes, although this could be varied.

HOW DO WE LEARN BEST?

This review activity can help you:[1]

- to start to think about your own learning
- to spot some things that influence your learning
- to see some things about yourself as a learner
- to lead on to a discussion of how to improve your learning.

☞ Review

1   On your own, think back to a past experience of learning where the experience was not a good one. It could be at school, in sports or in a hobby – but it was an occasion when you were wanting to learn and it was not such a good learning experience. Maybe you felt frustrated in the learning, or you did not learn what you wanted to.

Remember it in detail and then think about what made this not such a good learning experience. Write down the things that caused it to be like that. [3 minutes]

2   Now do the same for a *good* learning experience – where you learned what you wanted to, perhaps you enjoyed it a lot, were very involved, and so on. What was it that made the learning so good? Write down some of the things. [3 minutes]

3   In pairs, tell each other about the experiences you chose. Explain why the experiences were good or not.

Look for similarities and differences between what you have said. Are there some things that were alike in your experiences? Are there ways in which your preferences differ? [10 minutes]

4   In the whole group, collect up some of the comments everybody has made. Then ask how we explain what makes a good learning experience and what makes a not so good learning experience.

☞ Learn

Did any of the following areas emerge when explaining the good and not so good learning experiences?

- *Why* you were learning, anything about your *purpose*?
- *How* did you *do* it, the *strategy* you adopted as a learner?
- *What results*, the *effects* of your learning, on you and on others?
- *How* did you *feel* regarding this learning – before, during and after?
- *When, where, who* you were *with* for this learning, the *context* you were in?

Did you find anything interesting about your own or other people's learning?

---

1   Developed from Gibbs G (1981), *Teaching Students to Learn: a student-centred approach*, Milton Keynes: Open University Press

▷ **Apply**

Following this activity, is there something new that you want to try out in your learning? Which situation will you choose? When?

When will you discuss with others what happened when you tried something new?

TIME LINE OF LEARNING EXPERIENCES

This activity can help you:

• to think about your learning over time – the good and the not so good experiences
• to work out what made the learning good or not so good on different occasions
• to identify patterns in your learning and how the patterns have influenced your learning over time
• to see how you can develop and use the positive patterns in your learning.

▷ Do

1 On your own, think back to experiences of learning over the past five years. They might have been experiences when the learning was good or not so good. The learning might have occurred at school or outside school. Try and remember some of both sorts of learning experiences. [5 minutes]
2 Note down the experiences and how old you were when they occurred, using a table like the one shown here.

	My learning experiences	My age at the time	Score
a			
b			
c			
d			

and so on. [3 minutes]

3 Now give each of the good learning experiences a score between +1 and +5. Remember that +5 means it was really good!
    Give the not so good learning experiences a score between –1 and –5. [3 minutes]
4 Create a time line to show when these experiences occurred over the past five years. Mark the good learning experiences above the line and the not so good experiences below. [5 minutes]
5 Now, try to remember in detail what made the good learning experiences good ones.
    Was it to do with:

• *Why* you were involved in that learning, your *purpose*?
• *How* you did things, your *strategy*?
• What *happened* as you were learning, the *effects*?
• How you *felt* as you were learning?
• The place, the people, the equipment you used, or anything else about the *context*?

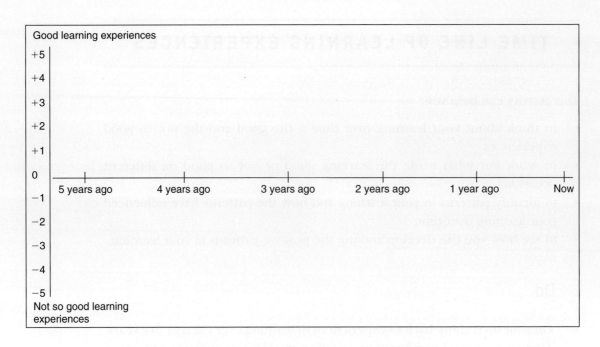

Write down some of the things that you can remember.

Do any ideas appear more than once? Could there be some patterns in what makes a learning experience good for you?

Then, do the same for the experiences that were not so good.

▷ Review

1 In pairs, show each other your time lines and explain the good and not so good experiences of learning and what made them good or not so good.

2 Then, point out any patterns that you have noticed and what they seem to say about what has worked well for you and your learning and what has not worked well in relation to the following.

Purposes Why the learning was important for you and what you wanted to do.

Strategy How you went about the learning.

Effects What happened or changed for you or others as you were involved in the learning or as a result of the learning.

Feelings How you felt as you were learning.

Context The people, place or equipment that you were involved with as you were learning.

3 Then, do the same for the learning experiences that were not so good.

4 In the whole group, collect up the comments and start to explore how *purposes, strategies, effects, feelings* and *context* affect our learning.

▷ Learn

1   Look at the various patterns of learning that you have identified in your own experience, using the ideas of *purposes, strategies, effects, feelings* and *context*. When did you seem to learn best and when did you not? How have the patterns changed over time?

2   What can you learn from other patterns that have emerged in your group?

▷ Apply

What ideas do you have about what promotes good learning experiences that you could use in your own learning?

Think of some learning that you would like to do.

From what you have learned today, what might help you and what might hinder you? Can you work out how to give yourself the best possible chance of succeeding with your learning?

LEARNING STRATEGY QUESTIONNAIRE

How do you go about your learning? This activity can help you to spot some of your strategies in learning, and then give you a chance to think about them.

▷ **Do**   Read each of the six statements below, and for each one decide whether you:

Strongly Disagree	mark under the column SD
Disagree	mark under the column D
Don't Know	mark under the column DK
Agree	mark under the column A
Strongly Agree	mark under the column SA

	SD	D	DK	A	SA	
1 I want to take only those subjects in school that would help me to get a job, not those that might be more interesting						a
2 I find that my school work can give me a good feeling inside						b
3 I try to obtain high marks in all my subjects because I like to beat the other kids						c
4 I tend to study only what the teacher says, no more						d
5 While I am learning things in school, I try to think of how useful they would be in real life						e
6 I have my way of keeping my books, notes and other class things so that I can find them easily						f

Did you find yourself strongly agreeing with one of the above six more than the others?
Which was it: a, b, c, d, e or f (see right-hand column)?
Now try some more:

	SD	D	DK	A	SA	
7 If I do badly on a test, I worry about how I will do next time						a
8 I say what I think is right, even though others may know more than me						b
9 I really want to do better than anyone else in my school work						c
10 I learn best when I memorise things by heart						d
11 In reading new stuff, I am reminded of things I already know and see them in a different way						e
12 I try to plan my work all through the school year so that I get the best grades I can						f

Again, did you find yourself strongly agreeing with one of the above six more than all the others? Which was it: a, b, c, d, e or f?

Give yourself:

| two points for a 'Strongly Agree' | one point for an 'Agree' | minus one for a 'Disagree' | minus two for a 'Strongly Disagree' |

Now make a total of your points in each of the six types so far on the chart.

Statement	Points	Statement	Points	Total so far
1		7		a
2		8		b
3		9		c
4		10		d
5		11		e
6		12		f

Here are a few more, to see whether there is a pattern in what you say:

	SD	D	DK	A	SA	
13 The only reason I can see for working hard in school is to get a good job when I leave school						a
14 I become interested in many school subjects when I work at them						b
15 I like the results of tests to be put up in class so that the others can see how much I beat them by						c
16 I prefer learning facts and details about things to trying to understand them						d
17 I like to form my own ideas on a topic before I feel good about it						e
18 I try to do all my assignments as soon as they are given to me						f

	SD	D	DK	A	SA	
19 Even when I have studied hard for a test, I worry that I may not be able to do well on it						a
20 I find that learning some topics can be really exciting						b
21 I would rather do well in school than be popular with my class mates						c
22 In most subjects I do enough just to pass, and no more						d
23 I try to relate what I learn in one subject to other subjects						e
24 I review soon after most lessons to make sure I understand what was taught						f

	SD	D	DK	A	SA	
25 Teachers should not expect us to work on things that are not going to be tested						a
26 One day I might be able to change things in the world that I think are wrong						b
27 I will work for top marks whether or not I like the subject						c
28 It is better for me to learn facts and details than to try to understand general ideas						d
29 I find that most new things taught in school are interesting and I may even spend extra time finding out more about them						e
30 When a test is returned, I correct all the errors I made and try to see why I made them						f

	SD	D	DK	A	SA	
31 I only want to stay in school long enough to get a good job						a
32 I believe that school should help me form my own ideas						b
33 I see doing well in school as a competition, and I am determined to win						c
34 I don't spend time on learning things that I know won't be on the tests						d
35 I spend my free time finding out more about interesting things that have been talked about in class						e
36 I try to read all the things the teacher says we should						f

Now make a total of your points in each of the six types on the chart.

Total from other page	Statement	Points	Statement	Points	Statement	Points	Statement	Points	Total
	13		19		25		31		a
	14		20		26		32		b
	15		21		27		33		c
	16		22		28		34		d
	17		23		29		35		e
	18		24		30		36		f

▷ **Review**   Did you have a preference for one?

Was it a, b, c, d, e or f?

Does this surprise you or not?

▷ **Learn**   Now here are some of the things which have been said about each type:[1]

a	People with a preference for type 'a' intend to meet the requirements which teachers put in front of them, but to do it just well enough to get by. These learners strike a balance between working too hard and failing. They think of their learning in terms of what they can get from it.
b	People with a preference for type 'b' study because they are interested, and because they want to get better at something, maybe some subjects. They learn because they are interested in it for its own sake.
c	People with a preference for type 'c' study because they want to come top and/or be seen as the best. These learners work to get the highest grades, whether or not what they are learning is interesting.
d	People with a preference for type 'd' study in a way which helps them reproduce what they have learned. They limit themselves to parts which are absolutely necessary, and memorise these so that they can repeat them.
e	People with a preference for type 'e' study in a way which concentrates on the meaning of what they are learning. They read around the subject, and want to connect what they are learning with things they have learned before.
f	People with a preference for type 'f' study in a way which gives attention to how they organise their time, their working space, and so on. They make sure they get things done, and behave like a 'model pupil'.

If you had a clear preference, does this description fit you as a learner?

---

1 Biggs JB (1987), *Student Approaches to Learning and Study*, Melbourne: Australian Council for Educational Research

- People with a preference for *a* or *d* focus on surface things and do well with those, but not so well when the learning gets more complex.
- People with a preference for *b* or *e* focus on the meaning or understandings and do better when they find learning is more complex.
- People with a preference for *c* or *f* focus on how to achieve, and get on pretty well at the sort of learning valued by schools.

☞ Apply

Think about some learning that you want to do soon. Would one of the preferences above be best for that learning? Can you practise using that strategy and see how it goes?

Talk over the detail of what you will try with a friend.

LEARNING STYLES QUESTIONNAIRE

This questionnaire is designed to find out your preferred learning styles.[1]
There is no time limit. It will probably take you 10–15 minutes.
If you mostly agree with a statement put a tick by it.

1	I like to be absolutely correct about things		T
2	I quite like taking risks		A
3	I prefer solving problems step-by-step, rather than guessing		T
4	I prefer simple straightforward things to something complicated		P
5	I often do things 'just because I like it' rather than thinking about them first		A
6	I don't often take things for granted. I like to check things for myself		T
7	The most important thing about what you learn is if it works in practice		P
8	I'm always looking for new things to do		A
9	When I hear a new idea, I immediately start thinking how I can work it out		P
10	I am keen on fixed routines and timetables		T
11	I take great care to work things out. I don't like jumping to conclusions		R
12	I make decisions very carefully. I look at all the possibilities first		R
13	I don't like 'loose ends'. I prefer things to fit into a kind of pattern		T
14	I get straight to the point in discussions		P
15	I like the challenge of new and different things		A
16	I prefer thinking things through before coming to a conclusion		R
17	I don't find it easy to think of wild ideas off the top of my head		T
18	I love lots of information – the more I have to sift through the better		R
19	I prefer jumping in and doing things to planning in advance		A
20	I tend to judge other people's ideas on how well they will work in practice		P
21	You can't make a decision just because it feels right. You have to think about all the facts		R

---

1 This instrument is based around the Honey and Mumford approach to learning styles, and is intended to give you a flavour of that approach. For a fuller look, please refer to the manual: Honey P and Mumford A (1992), *The Manual of Learning Styles*, revised edition, obtainable from Peter Honey, Maidenhead SL6 6HB

22 I'm fussy about how I do things – a bit of a perfectionist ☐ T

23 I usually come up with lots of unusual ideas in discussions ☐ A

24 In discussions I only put forward ideas that I know will work ☐ P

25 I look at problems from as many angles as possible before starting to solve them ☐ R

26 Usually I talk more than I listen ☐ A

27 Quite often I work out more practical ways of doing things ☐ P

28 I believe that careful logical thinking is the key to getting things done ☐ T

29 If I'm writing a formal letter, I try out several rough drafts first ☐ R

30 I like to consider all my options before making up my mind ☐ R

31 I don't like creative ideas. They aren't very practical ☐ P

32 It's best to look before you leap ☐ R

33 I usually do more listening than talking ☐ R

34 I can't be bothered with rules and plans ☐ P

35 It doesn't matter how you do something so long as it works ☐ A

36 I'm usually the life and soul of the party ☐ A

37 I do whatever I need to do get the job done ☐ P

38 I like to find out how things work ☐ T

39 I like meetings or discussions to follow a pattern and timetable ☐ T

40 I don't mind in the least if things get out of hand ☐ A

Add up the number of ticks for each letter.

Put the scores for each letter in the boxes below

A ☐   R ☐   T ☐   P ☐

Activist   Reflector   Theorist   Pragmatist

You will probably find that you are a mixture of two or three learning styles. If you have high scores in two styles, you are probably happy with both these ways of learning. If your score is fairly evenly spread, you are probably happy with learning in several ways.

▷ **Review**   Is the result similar to or different from what you might have expected?

☞ **Learn**   How does your profile of styles look?

Did you have a strong preference for one style? For more than one?

Now read the characteristics which are suggested for each style.

- *Activists* tend to be open-minded and enthusiastic about new things. They will try anything once and like to tackle problems by brainstorming. They are usually outgoing and like to be the centre of attention. They are well suited to working in projects, learning in groups and bouncing ideas off others. They may enjoy role-playing but may find they need help concentrating on lectures, writing up projects and analysing research.
- *Reflectors* like to stand back and think before they act. They are usually quiet; they like to look at the big picture on any topic and are very ordered and thorough. They are keen on listening to experts and doing background reading. They get a kick out of doing and using their own research, but are unlikely to be at their best when presenting ideas to a group.
- *Theorists* are analytical and love detail. They are hardworking perfectionists. They are the ones who take a logical structured approach and are quick at pulling together odd bits of information. They like lectures with plenty of theory and gathering views and opinions. Writing up notes and doing analytical exercises is their thing. They do not react well to uncertainty or people being flippant about serious issues.
- *Pragmatists* are very down-to-earth and keen to see if theories work in practice. They see problems as a challenge and they are always sure there is a better way to do things. They enjoy being shown 'how to' more than practising themselves. They are more tuned in to presenting ideas in smaller groups, writing up projects and using research data. They are weaker on tackling abstract ideas and background reading.

☞ **Review**   Identify occasions when you have adopted the style of an activist, a reflector, a theorist, and a pragmatist.

☞ **Learn**   Can you identify both strengths and weaknesses for your preferred style? And for your less preferred style?

Do your preferences for learning activities reflect your styles?

Most learning needs all four of the preferences at some time or other.

☞ **Apply**   Are there some of these which you wish to develop more?

If so, how will you go about it and who can help?

BELIEFS ABOUT SUCCESS

This activity can help you to look at your beliefs about succeeding.[1] Different people have different beliefs: sometimes they can help us succeed, sometimes they can hinder.

☞ **Do** For each of the 16 statements, mark whether you agree or disagree with them. There is space for you to note down your other thoughts as you go through.

		Agree	Disagree	Other thoughts
1	Sensible planning is a key factor in success			
2	Pupils who do well in examinations usually get a lot of help from parents			
3	Teachers only praise you to make you work harder			
4	When you fail it is usually because you did not work hard enough			
5	A regular study pattern usually leads to good results			
6	I need grades on the last test before I can plan what to work on next			
7	When I get things wrong it's because the teacher didn't explain clearly			
8	If you're told you aren't 'able' there's no point trying			
9	Doing well in exams is largely a matter of luck			
10	At my age it's difficult to study because you have to go out with your friends			
11	I usually seem to do badly when I have to compete with others			
12	People complain the exam was unfair when they didn't prepare for it			

1   Hamblin D (1981), *Teaching Study Skills*, Oxford: Blackwell

		Agree	Disagree	Other thoughts
13	There's no point to school if you can't get a job			
14	Progress in a subject depends on whether you like the teacher			
15	You can learn how to do better next time from your mistakes			
16	It's *who* you know that's important for success in life			

▷ **Review**   Discuss your responses with colleagues in small groups.

Look for similarities and differences between you.

▷ **Learn**   Which beliefs can hinder you? What do you *blame* when you do not succeed? How does this affect you?

Which beliefs can help you? How can you use more of them?

▷ **Apply**   Try and notice the impact of beliefs and blaming on your learning.

When this happens what will you do differently?

What do you know of examples that seem to work for you where you have managed beliefs and blaming differently?

HANDLING FEELINGS IN LEARNING

This activity is to help you learn about the feelings that can get in the way of learning. Some feelings can create a block to learning. This is because we feel things *before* we think and learn, so the feelings can stop us getting on to the learning.

> *Anna/Andrew are doing a maths task and realise they've taken a wrong approach to a problem. 'They've tricked me' they say to themselves, feel **angry**, and stop working.*

> *Anna/Andrew are practising reading for a class play-reading session. They imagine all the people looking at them, feel **frightened/anxious** and stop practising.*

> *Anna/Andrew are in class drafting a letter. They glance across at the next person's draft, notice that it has very neat handwriting and feel **ashamed** of their own. Pretty soon they feel like giving up.*

> *Anna/Andrew are carrying out an experiment. The liquid turns completely the wrong colour: they're so **surprised** they don't know what to do. They stop the experiment and pour the liquid down the sink.*

▷ **Do**   In your small group, decide which one of these brief stories you will look at first. On your own, read through and think yourself into Anna/Andrew's position.

As you come to the end, notice how you think.

- *Would you stop like Anna/Andrew did?*
- *Would you be able to carry on with your learning?*

▷ **Review**   In your group, spend a few minutes talking about what happened in the scenario.

Then make a list of:

- the sort of things Anna/Andrew could say to themselves to help them move on with their learning
- the sort of things Anna/Andrew could say to themselves which get them stuck with these feelings and stop them learning.

☞ **Learn**   When we feel something strongly it can get in the way of our learning. The way through is to think and talk yourself through. That way, you can move forward to do something.

Talk in your group about how this idea could help Anna/Andrew.

☞ **Apply**   On your own, spend a few minutes thinking about situations you know where a feeling can get in the way of learning. What can you say to yourself to talk yourself through?

Exchange your ideas in your group.

DEFENCES AGAINST LEARNING

Here are some things which people can say or think to stop themselves learning. Saying or thinking them reduces the risk that they will feel a failure (and also the risk that they will feel a success).

> *'It's boring'*
> *'What does it matter?'*
> *'I didn't choose this subject'*
> *'I'm doing all right in other subjects'*
> *'I can't . . .'*
> *'It's the teachers'*
> *'It's the course'*
> *'My parents couldn't do it either'*
> *'I had to do something else'*
> *'I'm only doing this because the teacher told me to'*
> *'What will my mates think?'*
> *'I've always done it this way'*

▷ **Do**

In pairs, choose some of the statements, and for each one discuss how it could stop the person learning.

Now for each one, think up what the person could say to themselves which could help them carry on with their learning. Example: *'It's boring – but it won't take long.'*

Try out your ideas in your pair.

▷ **Review**

Which things seemed to work, and help the person carry on with their learning?

Collect up the things you thought the person could say.

▷ **Learn**

You *can* get past these blocks!

Think if it might help:

- to spot them as they arise (which ones have you heard lately?)
- to remind yourself that you *can* say or think something different, to help yourself to carry on
- to practise what alternative things you will say or think.

▷ **Apply**

Think of a situation where you have said one of these recently.

Now what else might you say?

Plan when you will try it out.

Plan when you can discuss with others what happened.

EXPLAINING YOUR SUCCESS

People explain their successes in learning in different ways. This activity helps you to think about how you make sense of your success in learning.

▷ **Do**   Consider the following statements:

> *'I worked well at it'*
>
> *'I was just lucky'*
>
> *'I'm good at this subject'*
>
> *'It was easy work'*
>
> *'I had a good teacher'*

On your own, think of a subject you do well in and one you do not do well in. How would you explain your success in one? How do you explain your lack of success in the other? [5 minutes]

Did you use any of the above five explanations?

▷ **Review**   With a partner, think about the 'explanations' given above.

Which ones can you the learner control/influence?

Which ones are beyond your control/influence? [10 minutes]

▷ **Learn**   Discuss with your partner the following idea: people who explain their success (and failures!) by something they can control/influence/change in themselves are likely to keep going, develop further and achieve more.

Think of examples from your own learning and tell your partner about it. [5–10 minutes]

▷ **Apply**   On your own, think about one area that you are trying to improve, but it is not being successful at the moment.

Note down the explanations you are using at the moment to explain your lack of improvement. Are these explanations getting in the way? [5 minutes]

What else could you say to yourself? Things that you can control/influence/change by yourself.

Exchange your ideas with a partner.

LEARNING – IN SCHOOL AND OUT

The purpose of this activity is:

*   to think about learning in school and out of school
*   to make connections between in school and out of school learning.

▷ **Do**
In groups of four or more, each person in turn identifies two things they have learned – one in school and one out of school. Describe *how* you have learned.

*   e.g. My friends say I am good at helping them find what they want on the school's computer network. I think I became good at it because I've experimented a lot and was always showing them what to do. And so I learned more from helping them.
*   e.g. I play the piano. I had lessons for three years and I practised for half an hour most days. I really enjoy playing duets with my brother because we laugh a lot.

▷ **Review**
Are there any differences between what you said about learning in school and out of school:

*   *Purpose* – are there different reasons for learning in and out of school?
*   *Strategy* – do you learn in different ways in and out of school?
*   *Effects* – what effects on your learning do you notice in and out of school?
*   *Feelings* – are different feelings aroused in learning in and out of school?
*   *Context* – are there differences in the sort of places you learn in school or out of school?

▷ **Learn**
Did any of these come into your thinking about learning in school:

*   specialist facilities, equipment, knowledge available
*   structured learning programmes
*   groups of people.

Did any of these come into your thinking about learning out of school:

*   your choice of time, place, other people
*   different sorts of knowledge, facilities, equipment
*   you can be flexible, go at your own pace, go off at tangents
*   more control over time.

What others came to mind?

☞ **Apply** Make a list of other learning experiences you have out of school. For example, learning alongside adults or friends, practising sports, using computers, collecting things, jobs.

Can you use any of what you know about learning out of school to help you learn better in school?

Can you use any of what you know about learning in school to help you learn better out of school?

Try out your ideas in a discussion with a friend.

LEARNING SITUATIONS – IN SCHOOL

This activity can help you think in detail about the different learning situations you meet in school. And it might help you to get more out of them!

▷ **Do**   Compare learning in school in the following situations:

- two situations in which you are learning well
- one situation where you are not learning well
- a learning situation in school when you are not in lessons.

For each of the situations, think about the questions in the table and make some notes.

	Learning well 1	Learning well 2	Not learning well	Learning not in lesson
What situation is it? Where? Who are you with? Who is organising the situation? Who sets the agenda? In what way does the agenda include your goals? How do you go about the learning? How do you feel about the learning?				

▷ **Review**   What differences do you notice between the situations?

What similarities do you see in the situations?
Compare your answers with a friend's. Are they similar or different?

▷ **Learn**   Look at your notes and identify two or three ways in which the 'learning well' situations are different from the 'not learning well' situations.

▷ **Apply**   Can you use any of what you know about good learning situations to help you improve the not so good learning situation? Discuss this in a small group and decide what actions you might take.

LEARNING SITUATIONS – BEYOND SCHOOL

This activity can help you think about learning as a lifelong process – in other words the idea that learning does not stop after school! It can also help you in your skills of learning by doing research.

▷ **Do**
Design an interview to find out experiences and views of other people about learning in and out of school and after they left school, including learning in and out of the workplace.

What are they learning now? Where? Who with?

And how is it similar to or different from the learning they did at school?

Use your interview to talk to a range of people, for example:
- someone who has just left school
- someone who has had more than one job
- someone who is not in paid work
- a retired person.

▷ **Review**
What happened? Did you have any surprises in what people said about learning?

What did it feel like asking these people?
Did you think your interview got the information you wanted?
If you did the activity 'Learning – in school and out', did what people said differ from what you said in that activity?

▷ **Learn**
What did you learn from people's responses:

- What and how people need in order to learn at different times?
- How much learning people do after they leave school?
- How learning changes over time?
- Their view of learning?

What did you learn from this about doing research?

▷ **Apply**
What ideas are you having about your own learning after leaving school?

Redesign your interview to take account of what you have learned about doing this research. You might want to extend this research to more people or to ask more questions.

REVIEW OF LEARNING CHECK LIST

This activity can act as a useful review and consolidation, following explorations of a number of issues about learning. It can be used alone or with other people.

The purpose of this check list is:

- to explore learning about learning
- to help make connections between different learning in different contexts
- to become aware of changes that can result from learning.

▷ **Review**   On your own, spend a few minutes thinking about and making some notes.

What have I noticed about:

- what I find hard about learning, and what I find easy about learning
- any difference in ways I approach learning tasks that are set for me, and the ones I choose to do
- how I approach learning when I am on my own
- how I am able to use a number of different learning strategies or styles
- how I react to challenges
- how I feel when I have learned something new
- how I approach learning when I am with other people
- what I am able to offer in groups, for example, how I am able to help groups achieve learning tasks
- how I am able to encourage others to contribute.

If you are with someone else, exchange your ideas with them.

▷ **Learn**   Again on your own, consider the following and make some notes.

What have I learned about learning, for example:

- how my approach to learning differs from other people's
- how my learning strategies and styles have developed
- how I am able to respond to different learning demands
- how and when I am able to take risks
- how and when I am able to bring about any changes as a result of my learning
- how my view of my responsibility towards learning has changed
- how I am able to use feedback from others in the group
- how my approach to learning differs in different situations
- how working in a group affects my learning.

If you are with someone else, exchange your ideas with them.

▷ **Apply**   On your own, think about how you will use these ideas.

How can they help you in future situations, either when you are learning alone, or with others, in or out of school?

KEEPING A LEARNING FILE

Most often you will have a file for a subject, keeping the content of what you have learned. You can improve your learning by having a learning file, helping you look at the way you learn. Even when things are going smoothly, it is useful to pause and look at your approach.

Different people will have different thoughts in their learning file. For everyone, it can help you reflect, but again we all do that in different ways:[1]

> *'I'm used to keeping a diary to record thoughts, feelings, events etc. But I hadn't thought of using what I write to reflect and review. I'll keep it personal in the main – it's not for my teacher.'*
>
> *'It's a good change to focus on where I'm coming from and how I'm doing it, rather than just the content. But it's really hard.'*
>
> *'I disliked it at the beginning but I enjoy it now. As I moved on, I wrote about a wider range of things, and made more connections.'*
>
> *'I'm not sure about this idea of reflection – I prefer being active! The other day I came across some of my notes, and it made me realise how much I had developed. So I started some notes on that in my learning file. And then one thing led to another . . .'*
>
> *'It helps me remember that learning is about me and my development, not simply the acquisition of facts and their regurgitation.'*

You can reflect on your learning by discussing it with someone else, such as a friend. What you talk about may develop further when you have some time on your own.

How can I use a file to reflect and to record my learning?

Writing down your thoughts can also help reflection and learning. A learning file can be both satisfying and energising.

Some people find it works just to start writing in their file: then the reflections follow on.

Different people of course use different styles, write in their files different amounts at different times with different frequency, and sometimes do not use them for several weeks or months. Whichever way you do it, it will work best if you try to make a habit of the time when you write in your file.

It is best to think of your file as a means to help you learn. It does not have to be neat or 'written up properly'.

---

1   Thorpe M and Thompson J (1995), *Learning File*, 2nd edn, Milton Keynes: Open University

You could use your learning file to reflect on:

- a particular lesson or task
- connections between different activities or lessons
- your reactions to something you read
- important incidents in your learning
- any blocks you come across in your learning
- what you are learning about your approaches to learning
- what you are learning about the changes you make and the risks you take.

Reflection can be thought of as a conversation with yourself. So it can be useful to ask yourself some questions and try to answer them, to get the process going.

The following suggested questions may help promote reflection on your learning process.

- Why – your purpose in learning: *e.g. what is important to me in this work and why?*
- How – your strategy in learning: *e.g. which way did I go about this task?*
- Results – effects you noticed: *e.g. what helped me in this learning and what got in the way?*
- Feelings involved in the learning: *e.g. how did I feel when I started the task and how did that influence what I did?*
- Context issues: *e.g. how did I work with the group on a task? what resources were useful? did I influence the context?*

Another use of the journal is to become more aware of your own learning approaches.

Aspects of learning about learning[1]

- reviewing how we learn most effectively
- exploring our thinking and problem-solving
- reviewing beliefs about success
- exploring approaches to anxiety-provoking tasks
- acknowledging how the learning feels
- practising our approach to difficult tasks, talking ourselves through them
- examining responses to experiences of failure
- analysing contributions to group tasks.

What supports the writing of your learning file?

What inhibits the writing of your learning file?

> *Keep it simple, keep it focused and keep it short.*

---

1 Watkins C and Butcher J (1995), *Individual Action Planning: getting more from learning*, London: London East Training and Enterprise Council (LETEC)

BACK TO THE FUTURE

exploring and planning possible routeways to your preferred future

This activity helps you to think about where you would like to be with your learning at some time in the future. You can then begin to explore and plan the possible routes to your own preferred future.

Consider the following statement:

> *My future as a learner will be affected by what I think and do now about my learning . . . Therefore, I can influence the future now.*

What do you think of this statement?

It suggests that our futures can be influenced by what we do in the present.

▷ **Do**   Individually, spend a few minutes working on your own. Think of where you are now, and then go forward five years, to wherever you would like to be then: school or other places where you might be learning.

Where would you like to be up to with your learning then, and what are the things that you think you might be learning about by then? [5 minutes]

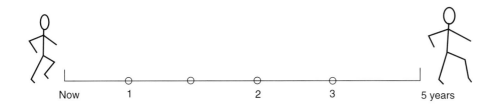

Now   1   2   3   5 years

On your own, note your ideas about the questions in the box.

> *What age are you now?*
>
> *What class?*
>
> *What year?*
>
> *What do you think about your learning now?*

What do you enjoy about your learning now?

What do you enjoy learning about now?

What age will you be in five years' time?

What are the range of situations in which you will be learning?

What do you think you will be enjoying about your learning then?

What do you think you will be learning about then?

▷ **Review** In pairs, exchange your ideas with your partner. [5 minutes]

- What will have changed about you as a learner over the next five years?
- What will you be enjoying about your learning in five years' time?
- What are the range of things that you will be learning about in five years' time?

Think about different aspects of your learning and how these might have changed too:

- How will your *purposes* for learning have changed?
- How might the *strategies* you use have changed?
- How might the *effects* of your learning have changed?
- How might your *feelings* while you are learning have changed?
- How might the *context* of your learning have changed? Think about where you might be doing the learning, with whom, when, and what equipment you might be using then.

▷ **Learn** There are probably a number of routeways for you to reach the goals you have for yourself and your learning. The routeways will be flexible.

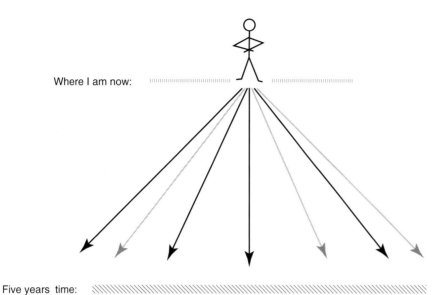

Where I am now:

Five years time:

Continue in pairs: think together about the varied ways and means that you could use to reach your range of learning goals. [10 minutes]

▷ **Apply**   Once again work on your own. In order to reach the range of goals that you are interested in, what aspects of your learning will you choose to develop? [5 minutes]

Think about:

- your *purposes* for your learning
- your *strategies* for learning
- the *effects* of your learning
- your *feelings* while learning
- the *context* of your learning.

Think about how you could influence any of these aspects so as to help you on your way towards where you want to be with your learning. Note down your ideas.

Then, in a small group, exchange the ideas and plans you have each had to help you on your way with your own learning. [10 minutes]

Section D

The wider context

- ◆ Parents
- ◆ Parents and learning
- ◆ The whole-school picture
- ◆ Developing a spiral curriculum for the whole school
- ◆ Pupil perspectives on learning

PARENTS

Parents have great impact on their children's views of learning.

Parents have great impact on their children's views of school.

When teachers talk about parents' role in education, or when they discuss with parents their children's progress in learning, it is very important to avoid any possibility of the 'blame game'. This happens when teachers and parents do not communicate well with each other, and do it all through the child. They are in a hidden competition of 'I'm best parent', i.e. my view is the best view.

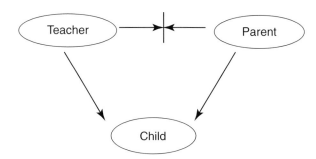

One way of avoiding this pitfall is to avoid typifying 'parents'. Find out which of the teachers are parents too, and bring their parent voices into the discussion.

The best way of thinking about productive relations between parents and teachers is to promote the 'healthy triangle' shown here.

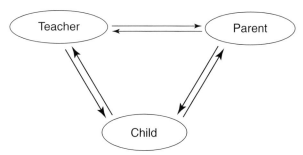

In this the various parties are clear that there are different perspectives and roles. They value the differences and feel confident to communicate clearly from their perspective, and contribute to the overall goal of enhancing the child's learning. Teachers often need to help parents to feel confident to do this, and/or to do this constructively.

Principles for both teachers and parents

- Recognise your common goal – the child's learning.
- Recognise the situations you are in – classroom and family.
- Recognise your different experiences of the child: they are not the same in both situations.
- Talk about your different understandings and the different contributions you can make.

Activities for teachers

- Explain to parents how you support learning in the classroom: ask them to consider this in their conversations with their child.
- Ask parents how they see the child going about learning: see if there are ways they know that the child's learning can be improved.
- Tell parents how you are helping the child learn about their own learning: ask them to consider something similar.

PARENTS AND LEARNING

Talking with your child about learning

There will be all sorts of occasions when you are talking with your child about something to do with their learning: it could be about something at school, it could be about homework, or it could be about their learning in a hobby, sport or other activity.

1 Try to include a clear focus on learning.

   For example, alongside congratulating your child for their latest achievement in their hobby, you might add 'Did you learn anything interesting about how you achieved that?' Keeping a specific focus on how the learning happened really helps. Another example might be when your child is talking about something which happened in class, even something which concerned them or frustrated them. Here again, as well as helping them find a way forward, it can be a real help to enquire 'What is there to learn from this?'

2 Try to allow that different people have different approaches to learning, and that they might all be successful.

   You might help your child by helping them notice how other people go about their learning: 'How does X do it, and is there anything useful in that?'

   Support them in trying out a new approach to a learning problem they meet, and looking out for what the effects are. 'Why not try doing it that way and seeing what you can learn from it?'

   And remember: how your children are doing their learning now might be different from how you did your learning. Take care not to fall into seeming to say 'Do it like I did'.

3 Try to help your child make connections across different occasions when they're learning.

   You might help your child by noticing how they go about their learning in some other situation you know: 'How would you tackle a problem like this in your skating?'

   You might include some of the dimensions of learning in your conversations:

why	purposes in learning
how do	strategies in learning
what result	effects in learning
how feel	feelings in learning
when, who with, where	context of learning

Talking with teachers about your child's learning

You have understandings of your child's learning which could be very valuable to a teacher. They do not know everything about learning. After all, they are in a strange situation – a classroom with 30 learners in it!

So whenever you get a chance to talk with teachers, do not hold back from saying what you see about your child's learning. Do not expect them to have the same view: they are in a different situation, so you do not need to agree with them.

THE WHOLE-SCHOOL PICTURE

There are many ways of helping learners learn about learning. Different schools may be helpful in different ways. There is no one way.

The ideal is that all our interactions focus on learning. But time is always scarce, so an overall vision for the school and some guiding principles may help busy teachers make the best use of time.

We need some ideas which keep the various offerings from different parts of the school contributing to an overall whole-school picture, and some ideas which help us decide what's appropriate for the different offerings, each with limited time.

What are the skills which learners need?

We can think of this at three main levels.

1 Specific skills, for example in a subject:
   • map-reading, using a dictionary, using an IT package.

2 Broader strategies, for example:
   • active reading for meaning
   • handling and organising ideas
   • constructing an argument
   • writing for different purposes and audiences
   • organising workloads
   • presenting work.

3 Learning about learning, for example:
   • reviewing how we learn best
   • exploring our thinking and problem-solving
   • reviewing beliefs about success
   • looking at approaches to anxiety-provoking tasks
   • practising our approach to difficult tasks, talking ourselves through
   • examining responses to experiences of failure.

You can immediately start to discuss:

• Which learners need which of these skills?
• Are there particular times/years when they need them?
• Are there particular contexts where they will need them most?

On the matter of which years might pupils need these skills, the aim is to create a spiral curriculum which revisits and extends skills year on year. When planning this sort of curriculum, and deciding what age to start, remember that we often fall into the trap of 'too little too late'. Pupils in the early years can take responsibility for their learning if the classroom is set up to support them.

Next you will see some draft ideas for a spiral curriculum for the whole school.

DEVELOPING A SPIRAL CURRICULUM FOR THE WHOLE SCHOOL

Learning about learning addresses themes which need to be revisited and built upon.

Planning to do that in a progressive way through the school years can be crucial for teachers' and pupils' perceptions of their learning.

There is no one way, but some possibilities for building a spiral curriculum are shown in the diagram. The intention is to move from the simple to the complex, developing increased sophistication of language and application each time a theme is revisited.

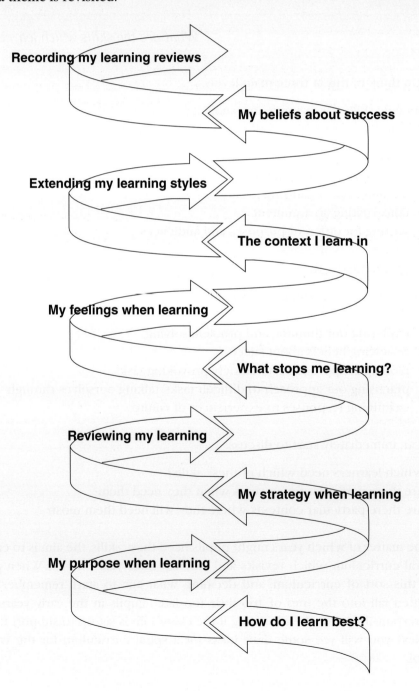

Recording my learning reviews

My beliefs about success

Extending my learning styles

The context I learn in

My feelings when learning

What stops me learning?

Reviewing my learning

My strategy when learning

My purpose when learning

How do I learn best?

What are the possible occasions for addressing these themes?

There are small-scale and larger-scale occasions, some of them planned, some unplanned. Examples could include those shown in the chart.

	Small scale	Larger scale
Unplanned	a conversation in the corridor	problem-solving in lessons
Planned	learning review at the various points in lessons	planned reviews in lessons, tutorials or PSE

In the secondary school, we also need to decide what is the best use of PSE or tutorial time and what is the best use of subject time.

As a matter of principle, it is best to teach a skill in the context closest to which it will be used. So we would promote subject-specific skills in the subject context. Some of the skills that apply across contexts are best promoted in a situation such as the tutorial, which looks across the contexts.

What does the tutorial occasion offer?

- the tutor has a cross-subject view of the pupil
- staff are engaged in a non-subject way, more free from syllabus demands
- the tutor's contact is a cumulative one
- the tutor group has a 'core' function among the various teaching groups
- the tutor has contact with parents and their view of the pupil.

Thus the following areas may be salient:

- overall achievement, recording a wide range of achievements and approaches to study
- how pupils are making best use of the school
- social and group relations, and any other issues which arise from the tutor's close knowledge of the group (i.e. a responsive curriculum)
- decisions where parents' views are influential (e.g. option choice, career choice).

PUPIL PERSPECTIVES ON LEARNING

On learning and working together

YEAR 7 GIRL: You learn more because if you explain to people what to do, you say things that you wouldn't say to yourself, really. So you learn things that you wouldn't know if you were just doing it by yourself.[1]

On responsibility in learning

INTERVIEWER: Do you set quite high standards for yourself?

YEAR 7 GIRL: I just say 'do my best' without setting any standard, because I think if I set a standard and I don't reach it then I'm going to be disappointed. But if you do your best and know you've done your best it's OK.[2]

Ask some pupils in your context about their view of learning and how to improve it.

---

1 From an interview with Caroline Lodge
2 Ibid.

Effective learning: a research review

◆ What is learning?
◆ What is involved? Models of learning
◆ What is effective learning?
◆ Effective learning in schools
◆ The challenge of effective learning: questions and reflections
◆ Notes for Section E

What is learning?

There have been many attempts to define learning: many of them can leave a reader disappointed.

The following definition draws out some key elements, all of which have individual and social implications for teachers and schools.

> *Learning . . . that reflective activity which enables the learner to draw upon previous experience to understand and evaluate the present, so as to shape future action and formulate new knowledge.*[1]

Features highlighted by this definition include:

- an active process of relating new meaning to existing meaning, involving the accommodation and assimilation of ideas, skills, thoughts and so on
- making connections between past, present and future which do not always follow in a linear fashion: unlearning and relearning play a part
- a process influenced by the use to which the learning is to be put, and whether the learning may be effectively retrieved in future situations.

This definition thereby makes a contrast with some prevalent views of learning, for example that it is a passive process of knowledge acquisition, with predictable and measurable outcomes.

A process definition such as the one above does not cover everything. It does not specify prior conditions (for example the process of learners selecting what to learn, the motivation and beliefs which the learner brings) nor the context in which learning takes place. Indeed, a definition of learning does not need to incorporate any reference to facilitators or teachers.

What is involved? Models of learning

A model draws out key elements and makes a statement of their relationship.

Dennison and Kirk[2] described the process elements, drawing on the model by Kolb.[3]

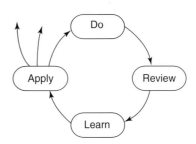

This model highlights activity in learning (Do), the need for reflection and evaluation (Review), the extraction of meaning from this review (Learn) and the planned use of learning in future action (Apply).

The process may serve for individual learners on their own who are actively making sense of a learning occasion, and for a group of learners involved together. In the latter case, time and support is required for individual processing to take place. A model which makes these elements explicit is given later (see page 99).

To address other elements affecting the process, such as the prior conditions, the context of learning, and the ways in which the process varies for different learners and purposes, the model developed from Biggs and Moore is useful (see p. 92).[4]

Note that this is not a linear mechanical model: the arrows denote influence both ways, recognising, for example, that outcomes affect characteristics of teaching, that particular outcomes for learning will accentuate particular learner characteristics, and that the qualities of classroom and school context affect the process of learning.

The remainder of this section is structured using the elements of this model. In the first half of the section useful ideas within each element are described. Then

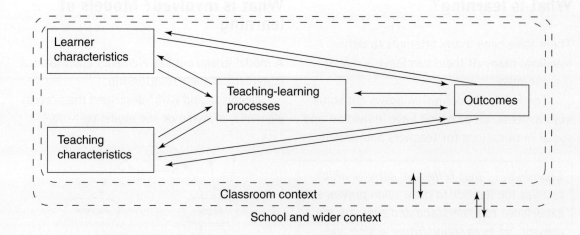

'effective learning' is defined and implications for each element are drawn out. Not all elements can be treated in depth.

Learner characteristics

Learner characteristics are not fixed: previous experiences, previous competence and beliefs influence the learning in hand. Learning occurs through multiple channels using multiple intelligences.[5]

Approach to learning is learned, alongside and linked to other core aspects of the person: gender, 'race' and so on, and is partly shaped by messages of value about those aspects, by family dynamics and cultural heritage.

WHAT STATE IS THE LEARNER IN?

	Unconscious	Conscious
	of a need to learn a specific skill or knowledge	
Incompetent	Unconscious incompetence	Conscious incompetence
Competent relative to a specific skill or knowledge	Conscious competence	Unconscious competence

Dubin has suggested that learners may be in one of four states depending on their competence and awareness of that competence.[6]

The suggestion is that 'conscious incompetence' is the ideal state at the start of a learning experience.

DO WE ALL LEARN IN THE SAME WAY? THE NOTION OF LEARNING STYLES

The notion of learning style as a general tendency has come to prominence in a range of different ways.

Students exhibit differences varying between surface-level and deep-level processing.[7] A surface-level style is characterised by memorisation of specific facts or part of the text. Students who adopt a deep-level style question the author's arguments and compare the evidence presented with the conclusions given. A third style has been identified – the achieving orientation.[8] This is characteristic of students whose aim is to achieve high grades (with or without understanding). Their learning style is characterised by playing the game to win and may reflect both deep and surface approaches. Some learners effectively identify the best strategy for making the most out of the institution in which they learn.

The term learning style is used by others to describe a learner's preference for particular modalities of learning (e.g. visual, auditory ways of processing).[9]

Honey and Mumford have developed Kolb's view and describe the following styles.[10]

Activists

- involve themselves fully in new experiences.
- enjoy the here and now
- are open-minded, not sceptical
- tackle problems by brainstorming
- constantly involve themselves with others.

Reflectors

- like to stand back to ponder experiences
- observe from many different perspectives
- value the collection and analysis of data
- listen to others before making their own points
- act as part of a wide picture which includes others' observations as well as their own.

Theorists

- integrate observations into sound theories
- think problems through in a step-by-step way
- assimilate disparate facts into coherent theories
- like to analyse and synthesise
- are keen on basic assumptions, principles, theories, models and systems thinking.

Pragmatists

- like to try out ideas to see if they work in practice
- positively search out new ideas and theories
- take the first chance to experiment and apply
- like to get on with things and are impatient with ruminating discussion.

An individual's overall approach may contain more than one of these styles.

ARE ALL LEARNERS MOTIVATED IN THE SAME WAY?
Learners vary in their beliefs about success, their motivation in learning, and their responses to difficult tasks.[11]

Positive pattern of motivation: 'learning orientation'	Negative pattern of motivation: 'performance orientation'
• belief that effort leads to success • belief in one's ability to improve and learn • preference for challenging tasks • satisfaction from success at difficult tasks • problem-solving and self-instructions when engaged in task.	• belief that ability leads to success • concern to be judged as able, to perform • satisfaction from doing better than others • emphasis on competition public evaluation • helplessness: evaluate self negatively when task is difficult.

Teaching characteristics

The characteristics of the curriculum, assessment and course design will impact on the process and outcome of learning. The teacher's conception of teaching also plays a significant role. See the School Improvement Network *Research Matters* no. 3.[12]

TEACHING WHAT? LEARNING WHAT? TAXONOMIES OF LEARNING
No single model of learning is appropriate to encompass all learning goals.

In Bloom's influential classification of educational goals in the cognitive domain,[13] distinctions were made between the following concepts:

1   knowledge
2   comprehension

3 application
4 analysis
5 synthesis
6 evaluation.

The six categories were portrayed as a hierarchy, with knowledge as a base and each level built on and making use of the previous levels. Development towards the higher levels of this hierarchy is similar to the development of deep-level rather than surface-level learning styles.

Much less quoted are Bloom's objectives in the affective domain.[14] This hierarchy highlights skills of:

1 receiving and attending
2 responding and engaging
3 developing personal values
4 developing an organisation of one's values
5 acting consistently with internalised and integrated values which characterise the person.

The division of cognitive and affective was always seen as an arbitrary classification, and no true separation of the two can meaningfully be made.

Yet in the mid-1950s, Bloom noted 'the erosion of affective objectives' from course practice, and described the way in which the cognitive bias in school testing, the slower rate of development in affective objectives, and the belief that the affective would develop without teaching had contributed to this erosion.[15]

Teaching-learning processes

To arrange activities which promote the process of learning is a complex challenge in any situation, and especially so in a classroom context.

The hyphen in the term 'teaching-learning' represents the core challenge of the whole teaching profession.

At a broad level, links can be seen

between conceptions of learning and conceptions of teaching, as shown in the table.

Conceptions of learning	Conceptions of teaching
1 *Quantitative* concerned with 'how much', essential facts/ skill	*Transmission of knowledge* communicate the knowledge (from an external source) fluently
2 *Institutional* concerned with validation of knowledge	*Efficient orchestration of teaching skills* focus on own techniques, management of resources (teachers plan in terms of their activities)
3 *Qualitative* active construction of meaning and interpretation	*Facilitation of learning* get students engaged in appropriate learning activities (what the student does most determines learning)

Methods of teaching are multiple, and a convincing categorisation of them is yet to be created.

Teaching activities are constructed from a range of elements, the central and cohering element being the educational goal, as shown in the model.

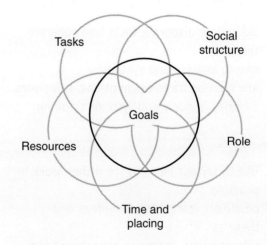

Tasks which promote learning processes are many and varied. A selection might include the following.

attend

absorb   listen   create

memorise   read   recite   model

think   categorise   tell   make   perform

analyse   describe   write   choose

question   present   replan   plan

judge   reject   discuss   draft   re-draft

deconstruct   let go   critique   brainstorm

debate   decide   prioritise   evaluate

relate   solve   communicate   integrate

review   negotiate   connect   synthesise

get feedback   give feedback   apply

experiment   rehearse

These tasks vary on a number of dimensions:

- from passive to active
- from individual to collective
- from simple and single to complex and multiple
- from surface to deep.

Outcomes

Outcomes of learning are not always simply measurable. Learning has long-term impact on people's views of themselves. Learning outcomes will include many of the following:

- knowledge – of things, people, action
- skills – with things, ideas, people
- action
- feelings and emotions – success, anxiety, risk
- a sense of oneself, including self as a learner
- a sense of others and of interaction with them
- ideas and strategies about learning
- affiliation to learning.

Classroom context

'Classrooms are crowded and busy places in which groups of students who vary in interests and abilities must be organised and directed.

Moreover these groups assemble regularly for long periods of time to accomplish a wide variety of tasks. Many events occur simultaneously, teachers must react often and immediately to circumstances, and the course of events is frequently unpredictable. Teaching in such settings requires a highly developed ability to manage events'.[16] Learners need specific skills to cope with the complexity of classrooms, and to become competent in conducting learning in such an environment.

Doyle has also shown us that in this context pupils and teachers may act to reduce ambiguity and risk, and therefore limit creative academic work.[17]

Many, or most, classrooms are associated with a profile of tasks which does not cover the full range listed in the section on 'Teaching-learning processes' (page 94).

School and wider context

Learning will be influenced by:

- the form of organisation
- the style of management
- the climate of relationships, between individuals and between groups.

School is the key site of institutional learning. It is a site for many constituencies in society to contest its goals. This can lead to conflict and teacher strain.

Some of the ways in which learning in institutions may differ from learning outside institutions are shown in the chart.[18]

Learning in school	*Learning out of school*
decontextualised	has 'real' context
second-hand	first-hand
needs motivating	comes easily
tends to be individualistic	co-operative/ shared
assessed by others	self-assessed
formal structure	few structures

We now move to define *effective* learning and consider its various elements.

What is effective learning?

The term 'effective' makes sense only when context and goals are specified. The present and emerging context have these important features:

- the knowledge base in society is increasing rapidly, and now doubles every four years
- in a society increasingly organised around the processing of information, more effective learners are required
- in a learning society, employment prospects relate more to the ability to enhance and transfer learning than the accumulation of qualifications
- people need to learn in an increasing range of contexts, not just the compulsory ones.

For these reasons it is essential that the goals of effective learning include the acquisition of learning and thinking skills: 'it is not enough to respond to changes that have already occurred. [School] aims and processes must anticipate future needs. These include learning to manage change and diversity, and developing the foundation skills for self-directed learning'.[19]

Effective learners have gained understanding of the processes necessary to become effective learners. This has been described as 'learning how to learn'[20] and 'meta-learning'.[21]

Effective learning 'is that which actively involves the student in meta-cognitive processes of planning, monitoring and reflecting'.[22]

Effective learning can be seen as a virtuous cycle, where effective learning promotes effective learning processes: the distinction between a process and an outcome decreases. In the contextual model (page 92), when learning is at its most effective there is

greater connectedness between the elements: the arrows of influence become more obviously two-way.

Effective learning in schools

How can schools, teachers and learners promote effective learning in their schools and classrooms?

We will examine this question for the main elements of the model on page 92, in a broadly reverse order to previously, and will conclude with a summary in the model on page 100.

Outcomes of effective learning

Effective learning is usefully described in terms of its outcomes and its processes.

Effective learning involves *outcomes* such as:

- deepened knowledge
- higher order skills, strategies and approaches
- action towards greater complexity and more learning
- positive emotions, excitement, enthusiasm
- enhanced sense of self
- more sense of connection with others
- further learning strategies
- greater affiliation to learning
- personal significance through a changed 'meaning of experience'.[23]

Effective learning involves *processes* of:

- making connections about what has been learned in different contexts
- reflecting about one's own learning and learning strategies
- exploring how the learning contexts have played a part in making the learning effective
- setting further learning goals
- engaging with others in learning.

A description of effective learning is useful in the task of planning teaching-learning processes.

Teaching-learning processes for effective learning

When planning for effective learning, the tasks and processes need to promote:

- active learning
- collaborative learning
- responsibility in learning
- learning about learning.

PROMOTING ACTIVE LEARNING

Studies of teachers' and pupils' perceptions of effective classroom learning show that they prioritise active approaches such as group/pair work, drama/role-play, storytelling and drawing.[24]

In the stages of the learning cycle:

- *Do*: the teacher encourages the learners to engage in a variety of tasks and processes. By favouring the active end of the dimension, engagement in learning is encouraged.[25]

- *Review*: the teacher facilitates and structures reflection on the activity and constructive feedback from a range of credible sources. Pupils evaluate affective as well as cognitive aspects: how they help or hinder the learning process.

- *Learn*: the teacher helps the students make the learning explicit, including through asking high-order questions to tease out new insights and understandings. The learning is founded in the reflection on the activity.

- *Apply*: the teacher helps the learners to plan future action differently in the light of the new understanding, by promoting transfer of learning, planning of strategies and goal-setting.

PROMOTING COLLABORATIVE LEARNING

Processing between learners leads to higher order skills,[26] so that co-operative cultures and group investigation methods give better academic results,[27] as well as improved communication skills and positive multi-ethnic relations.[28] These effects are mediated through the quality of group interaction, and highlight the need to promote learners' interpersonal and management skills.[29] For teachers trained and supported in groupwork, their role becomes more concerned with 'high-level' enquiries and freed from mundane tasks.[30]

Learner collaboration is encouraged at each stage:

- *Do*: tasks are designed to require collaboration; learners allocate roles and plan a group process.

- *Review*: students reflect together on the process in a suitably structured way, examining the interaction in the group, similarities and differences, roles and key themes such as power and influence.

- *Learn*: new understandings emerge about important processes in groups, how the individuals themselves operate, and the ways in which learning can be best enhanced through working with others.

- *Apply*: individuals can plan new strategies for this or other group occasions.

PROMOTING RESPONSIBILITY IN LEARNING

Classrooms in which learners negotiate an individual action plan using a study guide shows gains over high quality teacher-planned learning in terms of GCSE (General Certificate of Secondary Education) scores, retention of knowledge, and student reports of enjoyment, increased motivation and additional effort.[31]

Enhanced learner responsibility is achieved throughout the cycle:

- *Do*: learners negotiate areas of interest and development with the teacher, and then plan and organise areas of study. Action plans and learning contracts are made, using key skills of negotiating and decision-making.

- *Review*: learners assess their progress in light of the plan and examine what factors contributed to achieving or not achieving their goals.

- *Learn*: learners develop new connections and understandings through comparing and contrasting present strategies and approaches, and revise their plans for the next stage.

- *Apply*: each learner plans to approach new situations differently in the light of this new understanding and sets new learning goals.[32]

PROMOTING LEARNING ABOUT LEARNING
Three levels may be distinguished:[33]

- Level 3: approaches to learning
- Level 2: learning strategies
- Level 1: subject-specific skills.

A context which emphasises learning about learning leads to an increase in deep approaches and long-term improvements in academic performance.[34]

Promoting learning about learning demands that learners can discuss the tasks and processes they are involved in, and their own state in regard to learning.

- *Do*: using particular learning tasks, attention is focused on a learning process.

- *Review*: pupils evaluate the process of learning they have gone through. This includes affective as well as cognitive aspects, i.e. how emotional aspects help or hinder the learning process.

- *Learn*: a range of themes may be identified (below) and learners' strategies compared.

- *Apply*: each learner identifies learning situations in which they wish to try out new strategies and approaches.

Aspects of learning about learning[35]

- reviewing how we learn most effectively
- exploring our thinking and problem-solving
- reviewing beliefs about successes
- exploring approaches to anxiety-provoking tasks
- acknowledging how the learning feels
- practising our approach to difficult tasks, talking ourselves through them
- examining responses to experiences of failure
- analysing contributions to group tasks.

Learner characteristics for effective learning

Effective learners:

- are active and strategic
- are skilled in co-operation
- are able to develop goals
- understand their own learning.

HOW CAN WE PLAN FOR DIFFERENT LEARNING STYLES IN TEACHING-LEARNING PROCESSES?
There is no single view on how learning style theory should be applied to the design of teaching. Three broad uses are possible:

1   Part of a diagnostic matching of learning tasks to learners.

    This use is most likely when planning work with a small group of exceptional learners, rather than by everyday classroom managers.

2   Part of enhancing variety in teaching and learning methods, in order to reach more learners.

This use does not require the administration of diagnostic instruments to whole classes. Instead it reminds the teacher to plan learning methods which engage and extend the range of learning styles. Each may be engaged at different points in the overall process, for example activists, reflectors, theorisers and pragmatists would each come to the fore at different stages of a Do–Review–Learn–Apply cycle. A repertoire of learning styles is important for each pupil's future as a learner.[36] The cycle gives opportunity to develop each style.

3   Part of helping learners to understand their present approaches to learning and how to extend their approaches.

This use might occur in classroom reviews and planning discussions, as well as in smaller-scale events such as tutoring and mentoring.

Learning always has a private dimension, even when being promoted in a group context. Strategic learners are able to take themselves through the process of learning in a private way, even on occasions when the learning context may not be promoting such a process.

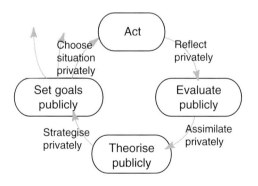

Teaching characteristics for effective learning

The term 'teaching characteristics' here means the characteristics of curriculum, assessment, course design and teacher's conception of teaching.

What teaching-learning fosters a deep approach? Gibbs suggests that strategies include independent learning, problem-based learning, independent group work and project work.[37]

External and institutional assessment strategies have to be matched with significant self-assessment, emphasising learner responsibility and control.

A curriculum which provides coherence for the learner will enhance the ability to make connections in different contexts.[38] Time and guidance for the learner to reflect on and make the connections needs to be provided.

Wood has described his vision of the classroom in the year 2015, in which the teacher will spend more time 'on attending to aspects of an individual pupil's learning processes'.[39]

Classrooms as a context for effective learning

Some analyses suggest that classroom climate explains more of the variation in learning outcomes than does ability or previous performance.[40] This gives added impetus to improve on the picture of classrooms characterised by low-level questioning and teacher-determined dialogue, thus missing out on the higher-order questioning so important for effective learning.[41]

Schools and the wider context for effective learning

Schools promoting effective learning will develop approaches which share the characteristics of learning out of school (see page 95). Connections with learning in different contexts will be promoted by methods such as investigations, action research and engaging adults other than teachers in classrooms. Such schools become learning organisations, and may exhibit the features below.[42]

FORM OF ORGANISATION

'Learning-enriched' schools encourage higher achievement by the pupils.[43] All members of the organisation are involved in a process of review, reflection and improvement: the teachers see themselves as members of a 'professional community'.[44] They anticipate future problems and seek continuous review.[45]

Curriculum organisation aims for coherence and connection for the learner.

Boundaries within the school and with its external community are undefended. Roles are blurred: teachers see themselves as learners, pupils see themselves as teachers.

STYLE OF MANAGEMENT

Leadership is shared and open, resource allocation is transparent and power and decisions are shared.

There is a high focus on effective learning.

The school and its key leaders model effective learning by encouraging evaluation, feedback, exploration and initiative.

Schools, through their form of organisation, can influence the feelings of efficacy of both teachers[46] and pupils.[47]

CLIMATE OF RELATIONSHIPS

The climate is one of high expectations, joint learning and shared responsibility for learning. Diversity is explicitly valued and the affective domain is explicitly considered.

The considerations of factors in effective learning are now summarised as shown in the model.

The challenge of effective learning: questions and reflections

The analysis of effective learning does not provide a simple prescription nor a recipe for easy change. As the traditional site of compulsory learning, schools may have initial difficulties in promoting self-directed learning. School learning is on the public agenda of many stake-holders, and schools are sites for public contestations of society's difficulties. 'A crisis in the school is a sign of a broader fundamental social problem'.[48]

For our future needs, we must ensure that our schools and classrooms emphasise effective learning as well as performance.

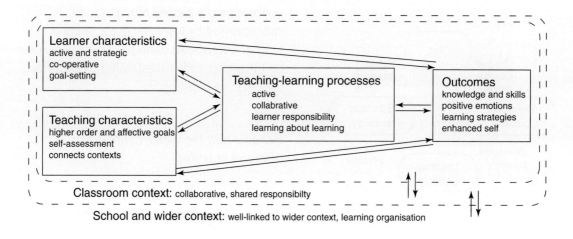

Review

Have any aspects of this section challenged your present view of effective learning?

What emotions and reactions have these ideas stimulated?

Can you evaluate these ideas with some of your colleagues?

Learn

In what ways can you review with your pupils their views about their learning?

What experiments can you plan to undertake in classroom activities for effective learning?

Apply

Do you consider that these ideas apply to learners of all or particular ages? To all or particular content?

If you have a policy on 'teaching and learning' does it reflect key ideas about effective learning?

Are you prepared to take the challenge of promoting effective learning even when it may seem like 'working against the grain'?

Notes for section E

1 Abbott J (1994), *Learning Makes Sense: re-creating education for a changing future*, Letchworth: Education 2000
2 Dennison B and Kirk R (1990), *Do Review Learn Apply: a simple guide to experiential learning*, Oxford: Blackwell
3 Kolb DA (1984), *Experiential Learning: experience as the source of learning and development*, 2nd edn, Englewood Cliffs NJ: Prentice-Hall; Kolb DA (1976), *Learning Style Inventory: technical manual*, Boston MA: McBer
4 Model developed from Biggs JB and Moore PJ (1993), *The Process of Learning*, 3rd edn, Englewood Cliffs NJ: Prentice-Hall
5 Gardner H (1993), *The Unschooled Mind: how children think and how schools should teach*, London: HarperCollins
6 Attributed to R Dubin; exact reference unknown
7 Marton F and Säljö R (1976), 'On qualitative differences in learning: 1 – outcome and process', *British Journal of Educational Psychology*, 46: 4–11
8 Biggs and Moore op. cit.
9 Keefe JW and Ferrell BG (1990), 'Developing a defensible learning styles paradigm', *Educational Leadership*, 48(2): 57–61
10 Honey P and Mumford A (1986), *The Manual of Learning Styles*, 2nd edn, Maidenhead: Peter Honey
11 Dweck C (1986), 'Motivational processes affecting learning', *American Psychologist*, 41: 1040–1048
12 Harris A (1995), *Effective Teaching*, School Improvement Network Research Matters No. 3, London: Institute of Education
13 Bloom BS, Engelhart MD, Furst EJ *et al.* (eds) (1956), *Taxonomy of Educational Objectives: the classification of educational goals – Handbook 1: cognitive domain*, New York: David McKay
14 Krathwohl DR, Bloom BS and Masia BB (1960), *Taxonomy of Educational Objectives: the classification of educational goals – Handbook 2: affective domain*, New York: David McKay
15 Bloom *et al.* op. cit.
16 Doyle W (1990), 'Classroom knowledge as a foundation for teaching', *Teachers College Record*, 91(3): 347–360
17 Doyle W (1983), 'Academic work', *Review of Educational Research*, 53(2): 159–199
18 Resnick LB (1987), 'Learning in school and out', *Educational Researcher*, 16(9): 13–40
19 Hayes C, Fonda N and Hillman J (1995), *Learning in the New Millennium*, Briefing New Series 5, London: National Commission on Education
20 Nisbet J and Shucksmith J (1986), *Learning Strategies*, London: Routledge
21 Novak JD and Gowin DB (1984), *Learning How to Learn*, Cambridge: Cambridge University Press; Biggs, J. (ed.) (1991), *Teaching for Learning: the view from cognitive psychology*, Victoria: Australian Council for Educational Research
22 Biggs and Moore op. cit.

23 Novak and Gowin op. cit.; Biggs op. cit.

24 Cooper P and McIntyre D (1993), 'Commonality in teachers' and pupils' perceptions of effective classroom learning', *British Journal of Educational Psychology*, 63(3): 381–399

25 Ames C (1992), 'Achievement goals and the classroom motivational climate', in Schunk DH and Meece JL (eds), *Student Perceptions in the Classroom*, Hillsdale NJ: Erlbaum

26 Wertsch JV (1979), 'From social interaction to higher psychological processes: a clarification and application of Vygotsky's theory', *Human Development*, 22: 1–22

27 Slavin RE (1990), *Cooperative Learning: theory, research and practice*, 2nd edn, Hemel Hempstead: Simon and Schuster; Bennett N (1991), 'Cooperative learning in classrooms: processes and outcomes', *Journal of Child Psychology and Psychiatry*, 32(4): 581–594

28 Shachar H and Sharan S (1994), 'Talking, relating and achieving: effects of cooperative learning and whole-class instruction', *Cognition and Instruction*, 12: 313–353; Cowie H and Rudduck J (1990), *Cooperative Group Work in the Multi-cultural classroom*, London: BP Education

29 Battistich V *et al.* (1993), 'Interaction processes and student outcomes in cooperative learning groups', *Elementary School Journal*, 94(1): 19–32

30 Bennett N and Dunne E (1992), *Managing Classroom Groups*, Hemel Hempstead: Simon and Schuster

31 Hughes M (1993), *Flexible Learning: evidence examined*, Stafford: Network Educational Press

32 Watkins C and Butcher J (1995), *Individual Action Planning: getting more from learning*, London: London East Training and Enterprise Council

33 Nisbet J and Shucksmith J (1984), *The Seventh Sense: reflections on learning to learn*, Edinburgh: Scottish Council for Research in Education

34 Biggs J (1988), 'The role of meta-cognition in enhancing learning', *Australian Journal of Education*, 32(2): 127–138

35 Watkins and Butcher op. cit.

36 Further Education Development Agency (FEDA) (1995), *Learning Styles*, London: FEDA

37 Gibbs G (1992), *Improving the Quality of Student Learning*, Bristol: Technical and Educational Services

38 Hargreaves D H (1991), 'Coherence and manageability: reflection on the National Curriculum and cross-curricular provision', *Curriculum Journal*, 2(1): 33–41

39 Wood D (1993), 'The Classroom 2015', in *Briefings for the National Commission on Education*, London: Heinemann

40 Haertal G *et al.* (1981), 'Socio-psychological environments and learning: a quantitative synthesis', *British Educational Research Journal*, 7: 27–36.

41 Gipps C (1992), *What We Know about Effective Primary Teaching*, London: Institute of Education

42 Senge PM (1990), *The Fifth Discipline: the art and practice of the learning organization*, London: Century Business

43 Rosenholtz SJ (1991), *Teachers' Workplace: the social organization of schools*, New York: Teachers College Press

44 Louis KS, Kruse SD *et al.* (1995), *Professionalism and Community: perspectives on reforming urban schools*, Thousand Oaks CA: Corwin Press

45 Resnick op. cit.

46 Hoy WK and Woolfolk AE (1993), 'Teachers' sense of efficacy and the organizational health of schools', *Elementary School Journal*, 93: 355–372; Lee VE, Dedrick R and Smith JB (1991), 'The effect of the social organization of schools on teachers' efficacy and satisfaction', *Sociology of Education*, 64: 190–208

47 Rudduck J, Chaplain R and Wallace G (eds) (1996), *School Improvement: what can pupils tell us?* London: David Fulton

48 Wexler P (1992), *Becoming Somebody: toward a social psychology of school*, London: Falmer Press

Section F

Further reading

- ◆ Key texts on learning
- ◆ Improving learning
- ◆ Future
- ◆ Important research articles

Key texts on learning

Askew S and Carnell E (1998), *Transforming Learning: individual and global change*, London: Cassell 0-304-33990-3

Biggs JB and Moore PJ (1993), *The Process of Learning*, 3rd edn, Englewood Cliffs NJ: Prentice-Hall 0-7248-1003-X

Boud D, Keogh R and Walker D (eds) (1985), *Reflection: turning experience into learning*, London: Kogan Page 0-85038-864-3

Bransford J, Brown A and Cocking R (eds) (1999), *How People Learn: brain, mind, experience and school*, Washington DC: National Academy Press 0-309-06557-7

Candy PC (1991), *Self-direction for Lifelong Learning: a comprehensive guide to theory and practice*, San Francisco, CA: Jossey-Bass 1-55542-303-5

Dennison B and Kirk R (1990), *Do Review Learn Apply: a simple guide to experiential learning*, Oxford: Blackwell 0-631-16838-9

Lambert NM and McCombs BL (ed.) (1998), *How Students Learn: reforming schools through learner-centred education*, Washington DC: American Psychological Association 1-55798-464-6

Marton F and Booth S (1997), *Learning and Awareness*, Mahwah NJ: Lawrence Erlbaum 0-8058-2455-3

Munro J (1993), *Learning How to Learn: strategies and directions*, Melbourne: Incorporated Association of Registered Teachers of Victoria 1-875572-40-6

Schmeck R (ed.) (1988), *Learning Strategies and Learning Styles*, New York: Plenum Press 0-306-42860-1

Watkins C, Carnell E, Lodge C and Whalley C (1996), *Effective Learning*, School Improvement Network Research Matters No. 5, London: Institute of Education

Improving learning

Biggs JB (1987), *Student Approaches to Learning and Study*, Melbourne: Australian Council for Educational Research 0-85563-416-2

Further Education Development Agency (FEDA) (1995), *Learning Styles*, London: FEDA 1-85338-390-2

Gibbs G (1981), *Teaching Students to Learn: a student-centred approach*, Milton Keynes: Open University Press 0-335-10033-3

Gibbs G (1988), *Learning by Doing: a guide to teaching and learning methods*, London: Further Education Unit 1-85338-071-7

Hamblin D (1981), *Teaching Study Skills*, Oxford: Blackwell 0-631-12533-7

Honey P and Mumford A (1986), *Using Your Learning Styles*, Maidenhead: Peter Honey 0-9508444-1-1

Nisbet J and Shucksmith J (1984), *The Seventh Sense: reflections on learning to learn*, Edinburgh: Scottish Council for Research in Education 0-947833-00-5

Northedge A (1990), *The Good Study Guide*, Milton Keynes: Open University 0-7492-0044-8

Novak JD and Gowin DB (1984), *Learning How to Learn*, Cambridge: Cambridge University Press 0-521-26507-X

Pressman H and Dublin P (1995), *Accommodating Learning Style Differences in the Elementary Classroom*, New York: Harcourt Brace 0-15-501741-1

Ramsden P (ed.) (1988), *Improving Learning: new perspectives*, London: Kogan Page.
1-850913-81-1

Selmes I (1987), *Improving Study Skills*, London: Hodder and Stoughton
0-340-39700-4

Future

Hayes C, Fonda N and Hillman J (1995), *Learning in the New Millennium*, National
Commission on Education

International Commission on Education for the Twenty-first Century (1996), *Learning,
the Treasure Within: report to UNESCO*, Paris: UNESCO 92-3-103274-7

Munro J and Munro K (1992), 'Learning styles: the way forward in the twenty-first
century', *Australian Journal of Remedial Education*, 22(3): 6-12

Important research articles

Bacon C (1993), 'Student responsibility for learning', *Adolescence*, 28(109): 199-212

Baird JR (1986), 'Improving learning through enhanced metacognition: a classroom
study', *European Journal for Science Education*, 8(3): 263-282

Biggs J (1988), 'The role of metacognition in enhancing learning', *Australian Journal
of Education*, 32(2): 127-138

Burns J, Clift J and Duncan J (1991), 'Understanding of understanding – implications
for learning and teaching', *British Journal of Educational Psychology*, 61(Nov.):
276-289

Cooper P and McIntyre D (1993), 'Commonality in teachers' and pupils' perceptions of
effective classroom learning', *British Journal of Educational Psychology*, 63(3):
381-399

Curry L (1990), 'A critique of the research on learning styles', *Educational Leadership*,
48(2): 50-56

Guild P (1994), 'The culture learning style connection', *Educational Leadership*,
51(8): 16-21

Haggerty SM and Aguirre JM (1995), 'Pre-service teachers' meanings of learning',
International Journal of Science Education, 17(1): 119-131

Hall K (1995), 'Learning modes – an investigation of perceptions in five Kent classrooms', *Educational Research*, 37(1): 21-32

Harris S, Wallace G and Rudduck J (1994), '"Coherence" and students' experience of
learning in the secondary school', *Cambridge Journal of Education*, 24(2):
197-211

Hattie J and Watkins D (1988), 'Preferred classroom environment and approach to
learning', *British Journal of Educational Psychology*, 62: 345-349

Hattie J, Biggs J and Purdie N (1996), 'Effects of learning skills interventions on student
learning: a meta-analysis', *Review of Educational Research*, 66(2): 99-136.

Keefe JW and Ferrell BG (1990), 'Developing a defensible learning styles paradigm',
Educational Leadership, 48(2): 57-61

Kember D and Gow L (1993), 'Conceptions of teaching and their relationship to
learning', *British Journal of Educational Psychology*, 63(1): 20-33

Leinhardt G (1992), 'What research on learning tells us about teaching', *Educational Leadership*, 49(7): 20-25

McKeachie WJ, Pintrich P and Lin YG (1985), 'Teaching learning strategies', *Educational Psychologist*, 20: 153-160

Marton F, Dall'Alba G and Beaty E (1993), 'Conceptions of learning', *International Journal of Educational Research*, 19(3): 277-300

Northedge A (1976), 'Examining our implicit analogues for learning processes', *Programmed Learning and Educational Technology*, 13: 67-78

Pramling I (1988), 'Developing children's thinking about their own learning', *British Journal of Educational Psychology*, 58(3): 266-278

Pratton J and Hales L (1986), 'The effects of active participation on student learning', *Journal of Educational Research*, 79(4): 210-215

Prawat R (1989), 'Teaching for understanding: three key attributes', *Teaching and Teacher Education*, 5(4): 315-328

Quicke J and Winter C (1994), 'Teaching the language of learning: towards a metacognitive approach to pupil empowerment', *British Educational Research Journal*, 20(4): 429-445

Rudduck J and Harris S (1993), 'Establishing the seriousness of learning in the early years of secondary schooling', *British Journal of Educational Psychology*, 63(2): 322-336

Säljö R (1993), 'Learning discourse: qualitative research in education', *International Journal of Educational Research*, 19(3): 197-325

van Rossum EJ and Schenk SM (1984), 'The relationship between learning conception, study strategy and learning outcome', *British Journal of Educational Psychology*, 54(1): 73-83

Wang MC and Peverley ST (1986), 'The self instructive process in classroom learning contexts', *Contemporary Educational Psychology*, 11(4): 370-404

This book was developed by activists in NAPCE, the National Association for Pastoral Care in Education, who also published an earlier edition.

NAPCE is the premier organisation supporting pastoral care and personal-social education. It is an educational charity, an association of schools and individual members.

Further details about NAPCE, its other publications and activities may be obtained from:

NAPCE
c/o Institute of Education, University of Warwick, Coventry CV4 7AL
Tel: 02476-523810 Fax: 02476-524110
Email: napce@warwick.ac.uk
Website: http://www.warwick.ac.uk/wie/napce/

Recent publications include:

The journal *Pastoral Care in Education*, published quarterly
Targeting Strategies - Hit AND Miss, 1998
Reducing School Bullying - what works?, 1996
Governors and Pastoral Care, 1996
Quality Review in Pastoral Care, 1996
Managing Behaviour in Classrooms and Schools, 1996
Refugee Children in Schools, 1995
The Value of Pastoral Care and PSE, 1995
Children and Bereavement, Death and Loss: what can the school do?, 1993
Whole School Personal-Social Education: policy and practice, 1992
Developing Effective Links with Parents, 1992
*From Head of Year to Year Curriculum Coordinator? A collection of resources
    for INSET*, 1992
Tutor Review, 1991

Send for a publications list and order form.

See also: Best R, Lang P, Lodge C and Watkins C (eds) (1994), *Pastoral Care and
    PSE: entitlement and provision*, London: Cassell/NAPCE 0-304-32780-8
    and Watkins C, Lodge C and Best R (eds) (2000), Tomorrow's Schools -
    Towards Integrity, London: Routledge/NAPCE